PureWool

SUE BLACKER

BLOOMSBURY

LONDON · BERLIN · NEW YORK · SYDNEY

A Quantum Book

Published in 2012 by Bloomsbury Publishing Plc
50 Bedford Square
London WC1B 3DP

Copyright © 2012 Quantum Publishing Ltd.

10 9 8 7 6 5 4 3 2 1

ISBN-13: 978-1-4081-7180-6

This book is produced by
Quantum Publishing Ltd.
6 Blundell Street
London N7 9BH

QUMPURE

Design: Louise Turpin
Managing Editor: Jennifer Eiss
Project Editor: Julie Brooke
Project Editor: Samantha Warrington
Assistant Editor: Jo Morley
Production Manager: Rohana Yusof
Publisher: Sarah Bloxham

Printed in China, by Hung Hing

The yarn requirements, knitted tension and other
pattern information in this book are correct
when using the appropriate Blacker Yarns. If
you wish to substitute your own yarn you may
need more than specified in the patterns and
to use different needles. We strongly advise
you should always knit a tension square before
starting to make a garment, especially when
using a substitute yarn. The information on
sheep breeds, including micron counts, is from a
variety of research but mainly from the practical
experience of The Natural Fibre Company and
may therefore differ from other sources.

Contents

Pure Wool

Pure Wool Philosophy

The importance of using pure wool from specific breeds represents a passion and faith, as well as a philosophy. There is logic behind this passion and faith. You may be reading this because you feel the same way, but it is worth going over the basics, if only to help you to convince others!

The Campaign for Wool and its patron, HRH The Prince of Wales, remind us that wool is:

- 100% natural: the fibre is not artificially made in oil refineries and chemical plants
- 100% renewable: sheep grow the wool every year for many years
- 100% sustainable: sheep live on land that cannot be managed and where crops and other animals cannot survive: high hills and fells, steep downlands, and, in some cases, even woodlands. For example, the White-faced Woodland sheep breed does not eat trees, unlike my Gotland sheep!

The logo of The Campaign for Wool (left) **and its patron** HRH Prince Charles (below left). **Baby Finley** tries a Blue-faced Leicester blanket.

- 100% biodegradable: wool will rot back into the soil. However, this takes some time, and it is possible to store fleeces for three to four years. It can also be recycled
- warmer: it both insulates and permits the passage of air, so it can keep you warm and still be breathable
- safe: unlike cotton, igniting at 255° centigrade, and artificial fibres, variously 420-560°, wool does not catch fire until it reaches 600° centigrade
- hypoallergenic: it resists dirt and stains and the accompanying germs, so wool needs washing less than other fibres
- a part of our historic landscape. Imagine Britain without fields of sheep
- being used less, partly causing sheep numbers to have halved in 20 years

Why wool for me?

Since learning to knit at around five years of age, and being involved with sheep since 1997, I have come on a long journey:

I discovered that all sheep owners believe their own sheep are the best, and they rarely have diseases or defects. I also discovered Gotland sheep. While they need a bit more care and are more suited to small flocks, they are determined to stay alive and healthy.

I found that sheep are intelligent with good memories (now the subject of research). One of my sheep, Jake, spent 30 minutes trying to break into the chicken house to get the grain, which suggests a degree of concentration – he was also working on the door catch, not any other part of the house. It's just that a set of teeth is not as good as a human hand!

I also discovered that wool is very rewarding, not just for the reasons above, but because it feels wonderful. There is a substance to wool which is hard to define. It is stimulating and rewarding to knit; calculating, experimenting, and watching the work grow. It is obvious to me, and now also to you I hope, that the arguments about and loveliness of natural wool should go hand-in-hand to sustain a future for both wool and sheep.

Somehow, I ended up with a breeding flock of Gotlands. I am starting to breed black Blue-faced Leicesters, and I run The Natural Fibre Company. This is not a lifestyle activity but a real business, with real people, products and results which are enthralling! The Natural Fibre Company is especially rewarding because its customers are so knowledgeable and interested in wool.

I also wanted to share what I have learnt. Finding the right yarn for a project is vital. The sheer versatility of wool and the possibilities of creating specific yarns for specific purposes are, perhaps, not fully appreciated. So we (the designers and knitters who made the patterns and samples, and everyone at The Natural Fibre Company) have tried to enable you to match the right fibre to the appropriate yarn and to a suitable design. We hope you enjoy it.

We hope this book will contribute to the history of farming, shepherding, industrial development and textile design in Britain, and bring some of this back to its roots in local provenance, quality and values.

Susan Black

Sue farms Gotland sheep and wants everyone to enjoy pure wool.

pure wool
basics

From farm to yarn

Sheep have been domesticated for 8,000 years, probably originating in the Middle East, then spreading around the Mediterranean and across Europe and Asia, reaching the UK 6,000 years ago.

The first sheep were small, multicoloured animals. Over the centuries they have been bred to give more meat and wool.

By 3,900 years ago, the British were spinning wool and weaving cloth. Exports to Europe probably started 1,300 years ago, and by the early 12th century, sheep and wool were central to the British economy. Innovations to speed up production were an important part of the Industrial Revolution in the 18th century.

The earliest known knitting – socks dated 1,500 years ago – are not truly knitting, but 'nalbinding,' a looped and knotted stitching made with a needle.

Examples of 13th-century knitted work have been found in Spain, but it was not until the development of steel wire in the 16th century that knitting could be done by everyone. Although the complexity of the early work shows that skills were of a high order and may have been evolving for some time, the remaining fragments do not give earlier dates. For crochet, the origins may be as late as the 19th century, but again this is unclear.

The sheep and shepherd's year

The sheep's year has changed little over millennia. Although some sheep can lamb naturally at any time of year, most ewes lamb in the spring. To do this, they need a ram 150–155 days before they lamb.

SPRING

Usually lambs are born from January to April. Some flocks lamb in the field and stay there, some shepherds bring in the ewes to lamb away from predators in the barn, and some bring in lambs born in the fields for a day or two in the lambing pen to ensure all is well.

Spring on the farm
Shepherds ensure the lambs are healthy and fed, but otherwise leave them to the care of their mothers.

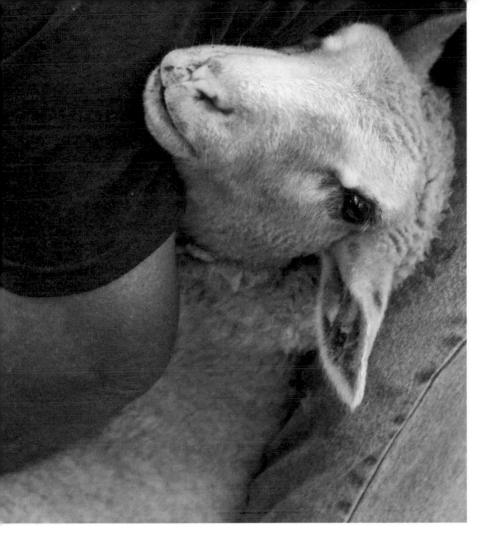

Skilled shearers are always in demand – the best can shear 250 sheep in a day. It's painless for the animals and essential for their welfare.

In the early evening the lambs race around the fields, playing, and then snuggle up to their mothers to sleep. Lambs start to eat a little grass and can be given extra rations to help them grow. The ewes may also need extra feed as they are making milk for their lambs.

SUMMER

This should be an easy time, with grass and lambs growing well, but a watchful eye is needed to repair fences, monitor progress, check and treat against worms, and vaccinate against diseases.

It is also show time! Agricultural shows across the farming world enable shepherds to exhibit their best animals, win prizes, compare notes and enjoy the sun (or suffer the rain, as the case may be).

For most flocks this is a time for shearing. In the south of England, this starts as early as May. As it gets warmer, the shearers move north and by August and September, the sheep in Scotland are being shorn. Many shearers travel the world – it can be summer all year round between the UK, US, Australia and New Zealand if you plan carefully!

AUTUMN

Now is the time for sheep sales: buying and selling ewes, rams and lambs to invest in the future and also sending the lambs and any cull animals to slaughter for meat and skins.

Once the sales are over, it's time for tupping: this involves bringing in carefully selected rams to work with the ewes for next year's lambs. The rams stay with the ewes for around six weeks and are then moved to a separate pasture.

Now the ewes are monitored carefully in case they need extra feed. Some ewes are brought in to stay in barns for the winter, or are provided with additional shelter, but most of the native breeds stay out, with perhaps access to a field shelter.

WINTER

For longwool sheep, there may be winter shearing. For sheep to be shown in the spring, there is shearing to get the fleece into the best condition for winning prizes (topiary has nothing to teach a sheep showman!).

Careful monitoring of the ewes, more vaccinations to give some immunity to the lambs when they are born, and extra feed if necessary are all winter activities. A cold winter will result in fewer diseases, but if it is a warm and wet year there is a risk of worms, liver fluke and even blowfly strike (see page 14).

From shorn fleeces to yarns

For the farmer, the end of the wool story is shearing, rolling and packing the fleeces into wool sheets – large sacks which take up to 60 kg (130 lbs) – then taking them to the local Wool Board depot, co-operative centre or wool mill. For the many smallholders, spinsters and craft workers who specialise in rare, minority or local breed wools, this may be the first stage of the job, although some people buy their fleeces at this point.

But it is only the beginning for turning fleeces into yarns and other products. Once at a depot or wool mill, the wool is graded and sometimes sorted to remove anything the farmer should already have removed (vegetation, dags, or poor, dirty or stained fleeces, all of which is better left on the farm for mulch and fertiliser).

Once graded, the wool is scoured (washed) to remove dirt and lanolin. Depending on how much it has rained, which breed produced the wool and where it was produced, the clean fleece will weigh only half to three-quarters of the original greasy fleece.

After scouring and drying, the wool is ready for processing. It may simply be teased apart, or blended with other fibres for colour or performance reasons. It is then carded to separate the fibre into a manageable and even web. Hand-spinners make the web into rolls to draw out for spinning, while machines create a number of individual slubbings, each one rubbed together sufficiently to be able to woollen-spin them on a large spinning frame.

If the yarn is to be worsted-spun, the wool is taken half-carded to a series of machines which align the fibres and comb out all short fibre and any remaining vegetation. This can also be done by hand, using heavy wool combs (such as those used to martyr St Blaise, the patron saint of wool combers and of a local church near my home in Cornwall).

As the wool is combed, removing air, worsted-spun yarns are less insulating than woollen-spun yarns.

The spun single yarns may then be plied to make a balanced knitting yarn, or remain single to wind on to cones for weavers or to be cone-wound and steamed for sock or machine-knitting.

Once complete, the yarns may also be dyed. Some yarns are made from fleece which is dyed after scouring, although dyeing finished hanks generally seems to achieve a softer result as far as hand-knitting yarns are concerned.

The original price of the wool, which by now is only about half the weight of the original greasy fibre, will have doubled in terms of raw material content of a finished yarn. It is then multiplied by 10 to 20 times (depending on the scale of machine production) for

The wool from Jacob sheep comes in a range of colours which can be spun into single-shade yarns, blended together, or even dyed.

Carding machines use a series of metal teeth to separate the tufts of clean, scoured wool into individual fibres ready for spinning into yarn.

The spun and plied yarn is wound into balls or skeins ready for sale. Dyeing can take place in the fleece or after spinning.

machine-made yarns, and a hundred times, although very rarely achieved by the craft worker, if hand-spun.

It takes an experienced hand-spinner a good hour to make 92 meters (100 yards) of yarn, after doing all the preparation by hand, so she will need three hours for a 3-ply yarn, plus an hour to ply it, to make around one 50 g (1.1 oz) ball of wool. Hand-spun wool is too cheap. And machine-spun wool from small, rare flocks, made in small amounts, is pretty cheap too.

Beyond yarns

Although it has been through all the stages from sheep to a yarn, the wool is still a raw material and has to be made into something – whether knitted, crocheted or woven – and so the yarn is the beginning of the third stage of the life of a fleece, after the farm and the mill.

Apart from single or plied yarns, whether woollen- or worsted-spun, there are many other types: specialist bouclé or single-twist yarns; dyed, marled; tweeded; yarns with glitter, wire, or different types of fibre added, and many more.

As noted above, the yarns may be supplied in several different formats. Usually, a knitting yarn is spun sufficiently only to hold the fibres together, to achieve the softest result (unless going for a specific style, such as a Guernsey yarn). Weaving yarns are made with a much higher twist for added strength so that they do not break under tension in a weaving loom.

Weaving opens a whole other world of technicalities and techniques, particularly the dyeing and finishing of a woven cloth, itself a work of considerable complexity. Could this be your next project?

Carded wool can be made into thin or fat wadding, called batts. It can be used just as wadding or made into felt using individual barbed needles or a needle-felting machine – or by using water, soap and muscle or machine power. Is this another project for you?

Wool can also be recycled by tearing up spun yarns or woven cloth in a garneting machine. It may be spun on specialist machines capable of spinning very short fibres, or used as wadding or carpet underlay. So wool is not a one-use product either! After its life in the third stage, there is a fourth stage of reuse, recycling, or composting to make nutrition for future generations of sheep.

Fibre facts

This is a very brief glossary of the terms used throughout this book. Together with the individual sections on each sheep breed, its special pattern and the section on Practicals, this should enable you to find and enjoy pure-breed wools, and use them successfully for your projects. If you need more information or clarification, you should be able to find out more about the terms used on the internet or by using some of the books in the bibliography.

In the Practicals section (see page 132), there is more information on knitting yarns and the differences in terminology between different countries when describing yarns. The information below is a very simplified guide and relatively personal, so you may find that others will describe things differently. This is one of the joys and challenges of sheep, wool, yarn and knitting.

Sheep terminology

AMERICAN LIVESTOCK BREEDS CONSERVANCY: a non-profit membership organisation in the US which works to protect more than 180 livestock breeds including sheep. It was founded in 1977.

BLOWFLY STRIKE: attack on a sheep by blue or green blowflies that lay eggs under the skin; after hatching, the larvae eat the flesh of the sheep. If not treated in time, this will kill the sheep.

CROSS-BRED: a sheep with parents of different breeds.

CRUTCHING: trimming off the fleece around the anus and tail to reduce the chance of infection and blowfly strike.

EWE: a female sheep.

EAR-TAGS: a plastic tag, now compulsory in Europe, containing a micro-chip to identify individual sheep. They cause problems in commercial flocks due to additional cost and time required to use them, but they are an essential tool in managing pedigree flocks. Sheep often lose tags, sometimes tearing their ears quite badly, by trying to eat stuff on the other side of fences and then catching the tag on the way back. It is difficult to replace tags in torn ears, though sheep do not seem to care much! Older marking systems, such as that used in Cumbria, consisted of placing notches in the ears to identify the flock owner and age of sheep. Some lambs are spraypainted with supposedly temporary graffiti numbers, which spoils the fleece as it does not wash out.

FLEECE: the growing or shorn wool of a sheep.

FOOTROT: infection in the foot of a sheep causing lameness; often starts with 'strip' or soreness due to damp grass, but also caused by numerous bacteria in the soil. It has a distinctive and very unpleasant odour. Can be prevented by using trace minerals and garlic, alongside good and careful hoof trimming, and can be minimised by good observation and prompt treatment.

HOG, HOGGET: a yearling ewe, north of England.

IN-BRED: a cross-bred sheep bred back into the parent ram.

LAMB: a sheep under one year old.

LAMBING: ewes having their lambs.

LIVER-FLUKE: worms that attack a sheep's liver, as part of a cycle from small snails, living in water courses, though the larval stage in the sheep. Sheep can survive this but it does not do their general health status much good and is best avoided or treated promptly.

MOORIT: brown colouring (there are many other Norsk colour terms; see Shetland sheep on page 115 for more information).

MULE: a ewe with a mountain or hill sheep mother and a pure-bred father, such as Blue-faced Leicester.

PEDIGREE: a breed society registered pure-bred sheep with (usually) at least three generations of pure-bred parents.

PESTICIDE: insecticide treatments to reduce the likelihood of blowfly strike or to treat it – fleeces treated with such pesticides should not be sent for processing unless there are at least three months between applying the chemical and the date of shearing. These normally contain dye to show they have been used and are not easy to wash out. It is also a growing concern that flies are becoming resistant to worms, but some alternative treatments, such as removing skin around the anus and tail to create hairless scar tissue (mulseing), are not considered welfare-friendly. This is an area of considerable debate.

PINKEYE: contagious eye infection, passed on particularly if feeding area is crowded. If not treated this can result in blindness, but it is easily treated with ointment – first signs are sore or slightly opaque eyes.

POLLED: without horns, e.g. the Cotswold is a polled sheep. Some distinct sheep breeds, such as the Dorset Horn or the Poll Dorset, come in horned and hornless versions.

ORGANIC: specialist, audited husbandry system designed to minimise environmental impacts of farming, for any farm product and processing at every stage.

RADDLE: coloured chalk worn in a harness by rams to mark which ewes have been served; will wash out of fleece.

RAM: a male sheep.

RARE BREEDS SURVIVAL TRUST (RBST): a registered charity set up in the UK in 1974 to protect and ensure the future of rare pigs, cattle, horses and sheep. The charity publishes an annual Watch List, classifying animals according to whether the population is viable or not without support. The RBST has been very successful in encouraging the rehabilitation and development of rare breeds, to the extent that many that were originally classified as endangered or at risk are now off the danger list.

SHEARING: trimming off the whole of a sheep fleece, usually done once a year in summer by professional, highly trained shearers. Shearing competitions do not judge only on speed; any injuries or poor treatment of animals cause a loss of marks in the final scoring. The world record for blade-shearing by hand is around two minutes per sheep, and with a shearing machine is under one minute.

SHEARLING: a yearling ewe, usually south of England.

SHEEP: generic name for woolly animals, originally wild, whose fossilised remains indicate that they have grazed in the British Isles for over 6,000 years. The first sheep appear to have been domesticated in Europe around 6,000 BC.

SHEEPSKIN: the skin of a slaughtered sheep – may be tanned and used for footwear, clothing and furnishing, and may also be treated to remove the wool, which can then be used for felt or, if long enough, for spinning. Sheepskin without any wool will also make a soft leather.

TUP: a male sheep, usually north of England.

TUPPING: putting the ram with the ewes.

WETHER: a castrated male sheep, used to keep rams company or to manage a few sheep for wool without lambing. Wethers live long and peaceful lives with few concerns except eating and growing wool. There are whole wether flocks specifically kept to grow wool (and possibly mutton) in some countries.

WOOL-SHEET or **WOOL-SACK:** a large bag into which shorn fleeces are packed for storage or transport.

WORMS: a problem to which lambs in particular are susceptible, although adult sheep can carry some and not suffer. Worm treatments have been over-used, resulting in worm populations being increasingly resistant to some types. More careful management is now undertaken.

YOW: a female sheep or ewe, usually north of England.

Wool terminology

Note: unless otherwise stated, micron counts are as defined by British Wool Marketing Board.

AMERICAN SHEEP INDUSTRY ASSOCIATION: represents 82,000 producers in the US. Started in 1865.

BRADFORD COUNT: old way to define thickness of fibres. Higher numbers mean finer fibres.

BREED SOCIETY: organisation set up to promote the interests of a sheep breed.

BRITISH WOOL MARKETING BOARD: set up in 1950 to collect, grade and market all wool from flocks of four sheep or more (except in Shetland).

CAMPAIGN FOR WOOL: set up in 2009 with support of British Wool Marketing Board, Australian Wool Initiative, New Zealand, Norway and Shetland wool associations and many organisations and businesses. It promotes wool worldwide and organises annual Wool Week.

COARSE WOOL: 35+ microns (my definition), better for carpets and felt than knitting.

CRIMP: nature of the curls, waves and crimps in a fleece.

DOWN WOOL: shorter, more bouncy, resilient and crimped, often non-lustre, 31–35 microns.

FELT: fleece or fabric where fibres are matted together.

FINE WOOL: 29–35 microns, usually down or lambs wool, but also native or minority breeds.

HANDLE: magical combination of softness, fineness, lustre, length and health of a fleece. Not easy to define – you know it when you feel it!

HILL WOOL: between mountain and down, around 33 microns.

LAMBS WOOL: wool shorn from sheep under a year old.

LUSTRE WOOL: wool with a natural sheen, around 26–35+ microns, often mountain wool.

LONGWOOL: wool which grows to over 4 in (10 cm) in staple length (my definition).

MEDIUM WOOL: 31–35 microns. I would add usually 5–10 cm (2–4 in) long.

MICRON: a thousandth of a millimeter, used to measure the thickness of individual fibres. Human hairs are 40–50 microns; sheep hairs start at 11 microns.

MOUNTAIN WOOL: longer, coarser, with more wave than crimp; 35+ microns.

NEW WOOL: shorn from sheep.

NON-LUSTRE WOOL: wool without a natural sheen.

SEMI-LUSTRE WOOL: wool with a slight natural sheen.

SHEARLING WOOL: wool shorn from sheep the summer after the year they were born.

SHORT WOOL: averaging less than 5 cm (2 in) in staple length (my definition).

SLIPE WOOL: from slaughtered sheep, mostly used for carpets. Unless label says 'pure new wool', some recycled or slipe wool may have been used.

STAPLE: wool fibres as a cluster; includes the length and the way the fibres hold together.

STAPLE LENGTH: the length of the wool from a sheep when straightened without stretching.

WOOL: the hairs that grow on sheep.

Yarn terminology

There are NO yarn standards – partly because wool is a natural fibre – and so this guide is approximate. There is no substitute for following pattern recommendations, tension swatches, and doing a few experiments. Once you are confident, start to knit and see where it takes you.

2-PLY YARN: a fine yarn making 32–34 sts and 40–42 rows for a 10 cm (4 in) square on 3.25 mm (size 3) needles. May be called sock or lace-weight!

3-PLY YARN: around 32 sts and 40 rows for a 10 cm (4 in) square on 3.25 mm (size 3) needles – similar to modern 2-ply yarns.

4-PLY YARN (UK YARN TYPE): originally made by plying four standard yarns together, as with

2-ply and 3-ply, now may also be a 2-ply yarn, two-thirds the thickness of Double Knitting. Equivalent to US Sportweight yarn. Around 28 sts and 36 rows to 10 cm (4 in) square on 3.25 mm (size 3) needles.

ARAN YARN (UK YARN TYPE): thicker than Double Knitting yarn, possibly 25–30% thicker, can be achieved by using two strands of 4-ply yarn, equivalent to US Medium or Fishermans yarn and Australian 12-ply yarn. 17–18 sts to 10 cm (4 in) on 5-5.5 mm (size 8–9) needles.

BULKY YARN: US name for UK Chunky yarn. Slightly thicker – 14 sts and 19 rows to 10 cm (4 in) on 6 mm (size 10) needles.

CHUNKY YARN (UK YARN TYPE): thicker than Aran yarn, around twice as thick as Double Knitting. Can be achieved by using two strands of Double Knitting yarn, 15 sts and 20 rows to 10 cm (4 in) on 6 mm (size 10) needles.

COUNT: the thickness of a yarn. May be measured in various ways, usually the thickness (metric count) or weight of a given length of yarn.

DEWSBURY COUNT: traditional standard thickness count for woollen-spun carpet yarns.

DOUBLE KNITTING YARN (UK YARN TYPE): originally a double version of 4-ply yarn but now commonly a 3-ply yarn, equivalent to US Worsted and an Australian 8-ply yarn, 22 sts and 30 rows to 10 cm (4 in) on 4 mm (size 6) needles.

FINGERING (US YARN TYPE): finer yarn, equivalent to UK 4-ply.

GAUGE: see tension.

GUERNSEY (UK YARN TYPE): a specialist fine worsted-spun yarn, in 5 plies, thinner than Double Knitting or Worsted, used for dense, highly textured Guernsey-style pullovers.

LACE-WEIGHT YARN: fine yarn used for lace knitting.

LOPI YARN: an Icelandic wool; not always suitable for wear next to the skin.

METRIC COUNT (NM): modern standard yarn thickness count.

PLY: the twisting of two or more yarns together.

SPECIFICATION: the definition of the particular thickness and ply of a yarn; can also include the number of twists in the ply or single yarn. There are no international or even national standards, so not all 4-ply yarns will be a certain thickness. It is important to remember this and ALWAYS KNIT A TENSION SWATCH if you need things to be exact.

SPORT (US YARN TYPE): finer than Double Knitting, 23–26 sts and 32–34 rows to 10 cm (4 in) on 3.25–3.75 mm (size 3–5) needles.

SUPER-CHUNKY YARN: a very thick yarn, usually specific to the manufacturer, probably around four strands of Double Knitting yarn.

TENSION: the number of stitches (sts) and rows made with a given yarn and given needle size to make a 10 cm (4 in) square. If you have too many stitches and rows, reduce your needle size and try again, or if too few, increase the size.

WOOLLEN-SPUN YARN: spun from carded slubbings, the fibres mingle in all directions.

WORSTED (US YARN TYPE): 20 sts and 26 rows to 10 cm (4 in) on 4.5 mm (size 7) needles, equivalent to UK Double Knitting and Australian 8-ply.

WORSTED COUNT: the traditional standard thickness count for worsted spun yarns.

WORSTED-SPUN YARN: spun from combed tops, fibres aligned and short fibres removed.

YARN: a thread made of twisted fibres. (In this book almost all fibres are wool!)

WPI (WRAPS PER IN): a useful way of determining thickness of a yarn and of comparing yarns by wrapping it around a ruler, not too tightly or crammed together (beware of very fluffy yarns when doing this!). On average: Lopi and Bulky yarns will have 5–6 WPI, Chunky 7 WPI, Aran 8 WPI, Knitting Worsted 9 WPI, Double Knitting 11 WPI, Sport weight 12 WPI, 4-ply Fingering 14 WPI, and 3-ply or Baby yarn 16–18 WPI. Remember pure-breed yarns may knit up in different ways because they are designed to give a different effect, and thickness alone is not entirely a good measure. Worsted-spun yarns tend to be leaner than woollen-spun, lustre and longwool yarns are also leaner, while downland, fine and short wools make bulkier yarns.

YORKSHIRE SKEIN WEIGHT (YSW): the traditional thickness count for woollen-spun knitting and weaving yarns.

pure wools
& patterns

Black Welsh Mountain fleece

The Welsh Mountain sheep has been prized for its meat since medieval times. The black strain has existed since the 19th century. It can live happily on the high hills of Wales without shelter or supplementary food, surviving in a landscape where no plough or cattle can go.

Welsh Mountain sheep are generally white, and are descended from a breed that dates back to the 13th century.

In the 19th century, fleeces from Black Welsh Mountain lambs (known as *coch ddu* or reddish brown, the colour they turn when they are bleached by the sun) became sought after. As a result, flock masters began to breed black sheep and created a separate, pure strain. The sheep remain black all their lives, unlike Hebrideans which turn grey with age.

However, as reliable black dyes were developed, the fleeces became less valued, and Black Welsh Mountain sheep less common. Recent concerns about the use of chemicals, interest in biodiversity, and the growing popularity of pure wools have helped this breed to become popular again.

Although these small sheep, averaging 45 kg (99 lbs) for an adult ewe, and 60–65 kg (132–143 lbs) for an adult ram, remain common in Wales and are popular with smallholders, the Black Welsh Mountain is not numerous. The Rare Breeds Survival Trust lists fewer than 3,000 registered ewes in the UK. There are approximately 800 animals in over 50 flocks in the US and Canada, where it is listed as a conservation breed. The North American flocks are the descendents of a flock of three rams and 13 ewes imported from Britain in 1973.

BREED AT A GLANCE

Sheep type: Native.

Appearance: Black fleece, long tails, no wool on their neat little faces and legs, as is typical of mountain breeds. The rams have horns, though the ewes normally do not.

Rare breeds status: Classified by the UK Rare Breeds Survival Trust as a Native Breed. American Livestock Breeds Conservancy classes it as Recovering.

Further information:
UK breed society: (www.blackwelshmountain.org.uk).
US breed society: (www.blackwelsh.org).

History: Initially prized for their meat, this pure and separate strain of black sheep was bred in the 19th century to satisfy demand for black lamb fleeces.

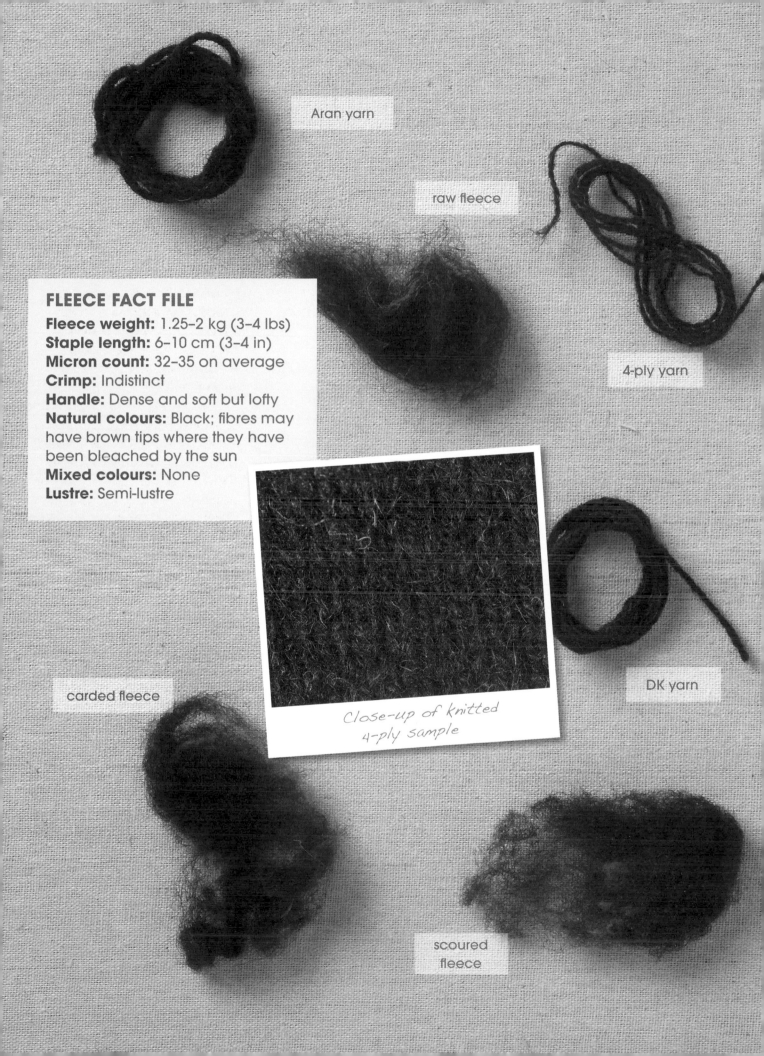

Aran yarn

raw fleece

4-ply yarn

FLEECE FACT FILE
Fleece weight: 1.25–2 kg (3–4 lbs)
Staple length: 6–10 cm (3–4 in)
Micron count: 32–35 on average
Crimp: Indistinct
Handle: Dense and soft but lofty
Natural colours: Black; fibres may
have brown tips where they have
been bleached by the sun
Mixed colours: None
Lustre: Semi-lustre

Close-up of knitted
4-ply sample

carded fleece

DK yarn

scoured
fleece

Black Welsh Mountain yarn

Black Welsh Mountain is a versatile, durable wool. Fleeces from lambs and shearlings will happily work as fine as a 4-ply yarn and right up to chunky weight. The wool is not generally suitable for wear next to the skin unless you are less sensitive than the average person (like me!). If you want to do this, look for yarn from younger fleeces where possible.

Black Welsh sheep have been bred to give a fine, soft and consistent wool. They rarely have coarse, kempy fibres. Lambs' fleeces are usually completely black, though older ones tend to bleach, resulting in off-black or bitter chocolate yarn shades.

Many white Welsh sheep (such as Welsh Mountain, the white Badger Face, and the Llanwenog, a Welsh valley sheep) tend to have black, coarse kemp hairs. It is this particular attribute that gives character to their fleeces, and it becomes more apparent with age. White kemp is more pronounced in the black Balwen, making for a heathery grey-black more suitable for weaving into rugs. If you find a Black Welsh Mountain fleece with more than a small amount of kemp it is probably not completely pure bred.

The yarn – which is soft and warm with a good loft – will cheerfully work in all types of pullovers, waistcoats, jackets, scarves, hats and mittens. It is also suitable for pillows, shawls and throws, and afghans. Being so soft, it might not wear as well as

Balwen or Badger Face in socks, unless blended with, say, 50 percent mohair.

The following pattern is for a unisex body-warmer or waistcoat, with a ribbed back to help it fit well and keep you warm. However, you could substitute Black Welsh Mountain yarn for the patterns included for Hebridean, Galway, Jacob, Manx Loagthan, Ryeland and Zwartbles yarns.

Versatile and cosy, the wool from young Black Welsh Mountain sheep (below) can be worn next to the skin while older fleeces bring stitch definition to outerwear (right).

YARN USER'S GUIDE
Good for ...
- Warmth, loft and bulk
- Blending and weaving
- Felt

Not so good for ...
- Inner garments
- Baby clothes
- Dyeing

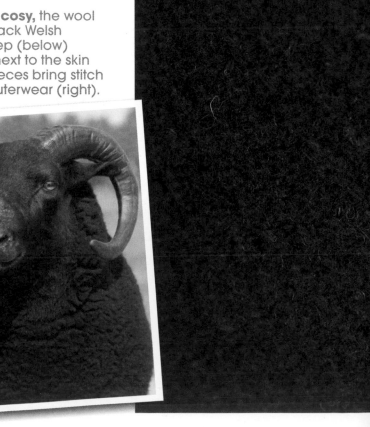

Cosy body-warmer

By Rita Taylor

This is a neat and simple body-warmer for children, men and women. It has an attractive moss stitch front and a cosy, stretchy rib back to make it fit well, so it needs no waist shaping. The garment may be left open as a loose waistcoat, finished as a true body-warmer with a zip right up to the neck, or you could use horn buttons or toggles and loops for a more casual/retro look.

For an even warmer garment, make two and sew them together to make a double thickness of fabric. Make them in two different colours for a reversible body-warmer, or use a contrasting coloured zip and matching blanket stitch for the seams.

Method

BACK (make one)

Using 4 mm (size 6) needles, cast on 70 (80, 90, 100, 110, 120) sts and work in k2 p2 rib until work measures 30.5 (34.25, 35.5, 37.5, 38.75, 41.75) cm (12 (13½, 14, 14¾, 15¼, 16) in). (Lengthen or shorten as desired.)

Armhole shaping

Cast off 5 sts at beginning of next 2 rows. Decrease 1 st at each end of every alternate row for 4 rows until 56 (66, 76, 86, 96, 106) sts remain.
Work straight until armhole measures 17.5 (19, 20, 21, 22, 23) cm (7 (7½, 8, 8¼, 8¾, 9) in) from decrease.

YARN REQUIREMENTS

Black Welsh Mountain worsed-weight DK
• Total amount of wool by weight and approximate length:
66–71 cm (26–28 in): 150 g/330 m (357 yds)
71–76 cm (28–30 in): 150 g/330 m (357 yds)
81–86 cm (32–34 in): 200 g/440 m (476 yds)
91.5–96.5 cm (36–38 in): 250 g/550 m (595 yds)
102–107 cm (40–42 in): 300 g/660 m (714 yds)
112–117 cm (44–46 in): 300 g/660 m (714 yds)

Shape shoulder

Cast off 9 (11, 13, 14, 16, 17) sts at beginning of next 2 rows and 9 (11, 12, 14, 16, 18) sts at beginning of next 2 rows. Leave remaining 20 (22, 26, 32, 32, 26) sts on holder (for back of neck).

RIGHT FRONT
(make one)

Using 4 mm (size 6) needles, cast on 36 (42, 44, 52, 56, 60) sts. Work in double moss stitch until work measures same as back to armholes.

Armhole

Decrease for armhole at left side only, as for back. Continue until armhole measures 7.5 (9, 10, 11, 12, 12.75) cm (3 (3½, 4, 4¼, 4¾, 5) in) from decrease.

Shape neck

Right side of work facing, cast off next 6 (6, 8, 10, 10, 12) sts. Decrease 1 st at neck edge of every row until 18 (22, 25, 27, 32, 35) sts remain. Continue until armhole measures same as back to shoulder. Cast off 9 (11, 13, 14, 16, 17) sts at beginning next row and 9

MEASUREMENTS

Around the bust: 66–71 (71–76, 81–86, 91.5–96.5, 102–107, 112–117) cm (26–28 (28–30, 32–34, 36–38, 40–42, 44–46) in)
Garment measurement: 71–76 (76–81, 86–91, 96.5–101.5, 107–112, 117–122) cm (28–30 (30–32, 34–36, 38–40, 42–44, 46–48) in)
Length: 48 (51, 53.5, 56, 58.5, 61, 63) cm (19 (21, 22, 23, 24, 25) in)
Instructions are given for the smallest size first, followed by larger sizes in brackets

NEEDLES & NOTIONS

One pair each 3.5 mm (size 4) and 4 mm (size 6) knitting needles
Stitch holder
Zip or toggles/buttons (optional)

TENSION

Approx 20 sts x 28 rows = 10cm (4 in) over stocking stitch on 4 mm (size 6) needles
Adjust needle size to give required tension.

ABBREVIATIONS (see also page 140)
Double moss stitch: Rows 1 and 2: (k2 p2) to end; Rows 3 and 4: (p2, k2) to end.

(11, 12, 14, 16, 18) sts at beginning of following alternate row

LEFT FRONT
(make one)

Work as for right front, reversing shapings.

SHOULDER SEAMS

Sew fronts to back along shoulder seams.

NECKBAND

Using 3.5 mm (size 4) needles, pick up and k across 6 (6, 8, 10, 10, 12) sts cast off for neck, pick up and knit 16 (18, 20, 22, 24, 26) sts from right front neck edge, knit 20 (22, 26, 32, 32, 26) sts from stitch holder at back neck, pick up and knit 16 (18, 20, 22, 24, 26) sts from left front neck edge, pick up and knit 6 (6, 8, 10, 10, 12) sts from cast off sts at left neck edge. Work 6 rows in K2 P2 rib. Cast off.

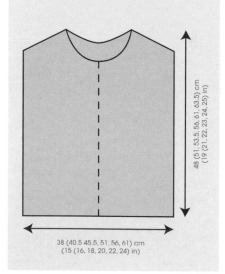

To fit sizes 66–71 (71–76, 81–86, 91.5–96.5, 102–107, 112–117) cm (26–28 (28–30, 32–34, 36–38, 40–42, 44–46) in)

48 (51, 53.5, 56, 61, 63.5) cm (19 (21, 22, 23, 24, 25) in)

38 (40.5 45.5, 51, 56, 61) cm (15 (16, 18, 20, 22, 24) in)

FINISHING

Sew side seams. Sew in zip or make loops for toggles and sew on toggles. Darn in all loose ends.

Blue-faced Leicester fleece

The Blue-faced Leicester was originally concentrated in the north of England and known as the Hexham Leicester. It is a big, tall sheep, with a very fine long fleece, hanging distinctively in individual neat locks with a tiny crimp. It has no wool on the head and legs, virtually none on the belly, and it does not have the top-knot or fringe typical of the Leicester or Lincoln Longwool.

The fleece of the Blue-faced Leicester is prized for its ability to produce fine, soft, hard-wearing and lustrous yarns. The wool is fine and dense, and spins into a soft yarn.

The sheep has a wide chest, and a long straight back, with the appearance of a square body and legs at the corners. It has the typical Roman nose of the Leicester breed and big hare-like ears.

If left a bit later for shearing, the fleeces peel back from the necks and, to my mind, give these sheep a slightly vulture-like appearance!

The ewes weigh in at around 80 kg (176 lbs) and the rams at 115 kg (253 lbs), making them one of the largest British sheep breeds.

The Blue-faced Leicester is now mainly bred to create 'terminal sire' pedigree rams to cross with mountain sheep. The resulting progeny are known as 'Mules'.

Mule ewes produce strong, fast-growing lambs, while maintaining their dam's hardiness and longevity. Today Mules number half of all crossbred ewes in the UK.

The Blue-faced Leicester is not rare, though it might have a natural tendency to be rare, as it is not known for its hardiness, and some (perhaps prejudiced?) people say all purchases of one of these wonderful sheep should have a spade thrown in for use at burial!

However, it has wider appeal. The first Blue-faced Leicester were imported into Canada in 1970 and the first flocks appeared in the US in the 1980s.

BREED AT A GLANCE

Sheep type: Native.
Appearance: Creamy white, with grey skin on the head (hence the name Blue-faced) and an occasional tendency to produce 'black' versions. Hornless with a long tail.
Rare breeds status: None.
Further information:
UK breed society: www.blueleicester.co.uk.
US breed societies: www.bflba.com, www.bflsheep.com.
History: The Blue-faced Leicester is a relatively recent sheep. Development was started in 18th-century Leicestershire, UK, by Robert Bakewell, as part of his programme to breed longwooled sheep, and continued in Northumberland into the early 20th century.

4-ply yarn

raw fleece

FLEECE FACT FILE
Fleece weight: 1–2 kg (2.2–4.4 lbs)
Staple length: 8–15cm (3–6 in)
Micron count: 26–26.5
Crimp: Fine
Handle: Silky
Natural colours: White, some black and grey
Mixed colours: None
Lustre: Semi-lustre

scoured
fleece

Close-up of knitted 4-ply sample

carded fleece

DK yarn

Blue-faced Leicester yarn

The drapey, heavy wool of the Blue-faced Leicester sheep makes one of the most popular knitting yarns for those who love soft wool. It is a buttery golden cream in colour and has an almost soapy soft texture.

The wool of the Blue-faced Leicester is amongst the finest produced in the UK and is very consistent across the whole body, with no kemp. Due to the fine crimp, the locks appear to be quite short, but stretch out to a staple length of 8–15 cm (3–6 in). It is a very dense fibre, so a small sack will weigh a lot more than one of a similar size containing, say, fleece from Ryeland or Shetland sheep.

Despite its renowned softness, as a semi-lustre wool, the yarn made from Blue-faced Leicester sheep is also reasonably hard-wearing. When worsted-spun it also has a lovely sheen and, of course, it dyes well too. As a result the wool is excellent to add to weaving yarns in blends to achieve some lustre, dye-friendliness and drape, and can, for example, be used to maintain the characteristics of mohair yarn, while making adult mohair fibre softer and easier to spin.

Despite their size, Blue-faced Leicesters produce fleeces half the weight of other Leicester breeds. This, and the bare belly, may explain their lack of hardiness. If you are lucky enough to find some 'black' fibre, it will not be black at all, but a rich chocolate brown as the fleece bleaches quite heavily in the sun. In fact, a 'black' Blue-faced Leicester sheep will only look black around the edges.

The lustre of Blue-faced Leicester yarns makes them perfect for textured knitting, as it will emphasise the stitches. Here, we have also taken advantage of its softness to create a baby blanket with a geometric design, and a lacy ladies' sleeveless top. If you want to try other options, substitute Blue-faced Leicester yarn for the patterns shown for Castlemilk Moorit, Corriedale, Gotland or Manx Loagthan yarns.

Soft and lustrous yarn spun from the fleece of Blue-faced Leicester sheep is ideal for textured stitches and lace knitting where it shows the stitches and openwork patterns to great effect. The knitted garments also drape well.

Scallop shell top
By Rita Taylor

The lacy scallop shell pattern of this sleeveless top is deceptively simple to knit, and the square neckline and garter stitch edges mean there are no tricky decrease rows. Generous side slits make it comfortable to wear.

It knits up well in Blue-faced Leicester or an alpaca or alpaca/Shetland yarn.

Method

Tip: To make a neat edge, cast on 2 extra stitches and ALWAYS slip the first stitch and knit or purl the last stitch of every row (but remember to include these stitches when counting for decreases).

SCALLOP SHELL PATTERN

Pattern worked over 15 sts and 12 rows:

Row 1: (k5, k2tog, yf, k1, yf, ssk, k5)

Row 2 and every even row: (p15)

Row 3: (k4, k2tog, k1, yf, k1, yf, k1, ssk, k4)

Row 5: (k3, k2tog, k2, yf, k1, yf, k2, ssk, k3)

Row 7: (k2, k2tog, k3, yf, k1, yf, k3, ssk, k2)

Row 9: (k1, k2tog, k4, yf, k1, yf, k4, ssk, k1)

Row 11: (k2tog, k5, yf, k1, yf, k5, ssk)

Row 12: as row 2

BACK (make 1)

Cast on 89 (106, 123) sts on 3.75 mm (size 5) needles. Work in garter stitch for 6 rows increasing 1 st at each end of last row to 91 (108, 125) sts.

Change to size 6 (4 mm) needles and work scallop shells pattern with garter stitch edges and 2 knit sts between each scallop. Therefore:

Row 1: K4, *pattern row 1, k2*

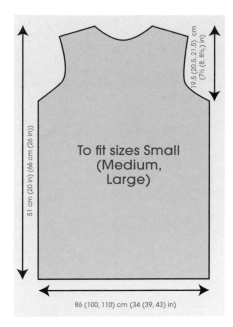

To fit sizes Small (Medium, Large)

51 cm (20 in) (66 cm (26 in))

19.5 (20.5, 21.5) cm (7½ (8, 8½) in)

86 (100, 110) cm (34, 39, 43) in)

FINISHED SIZES
Garment size: chest 86 (100, 110) cm (34 (39, 43) in); length (neck to hem) 51 cm (20 in) (66 cm (26 in)) for longer version
Instructions are given for the smallest size first, followed by medium and large in brackets.

NEEDLES & NOTIONS
1 pair needles 4 mm (size 6)
1 pair needles 3.75 mm (size 5)
3 stitch holders
Safety pin

TENSION
Approx 23 sts x 29 rows = 10 cm (4 in) over scallop shell pattern on 4 mm (size 6) needles.
Adjust needle size to give required tension

ABBREVIATIONS (see also page 140)
ssk: (slip, slip, knit) slip 2 stitches knitwise from the left to the right needle, then insert the tip of the left needle into the fronts of the slipped stitches and knit them together from this position.

SKILL LEVEL

repeat to last 2 sts, k2.
Row 2: K4 *pattern row 2, k2* repeat to last 2 sts, k2.
Thus, the small size will have five scallop pattern repeats, the medium size will have six and the large size will have seven across the width of the garment, plus the 2 k sts between each scallop and the knit stitches at the edges.
Continue with pattern as set until seven patterns repeats have been worked (ten for the longer version).

Armhole shaping
Cast off 7 sts, k14, pattern to last 21 sts, knit to end.
Cast off 7 sts, pattern to end, keeping 2 k sts on either side of scallops. (77 (94, 111) sts).
Working first and last pattern repeats in st st (so that you only have 3 (4, 5) scallops, each with 2 k sts between), decrease on alternate rows as follows:
Row 1: K1, ssk, work to last 3 sts, k2tog, k1.
Row 2: work in pattern as set.
Repeat these 2 rows 4 times (67 (84, 101) sts).
Continue as set, keeping edge sts in st st until armholes measure 18 (19, 20) cm (7 (7½, 8,) in).

Shoulder shaping
Cast off 8 (12, 14) sts at beginning of next 2 rows and 9 (12, 14) sts at beginning of following 2 rows. Leave remaining 33 (36, 45) sts on holder for back neck.

FRONT (make 1)
Work as for back until armholes measure (11 (13, 14) cm 4½ (5, 5½) in, ending with a WS row.

Neck shaping:
Pattern 23 (30, 38) sts, place 21 (24, 25) sts on holder, then pattern to end (24 (31, 38) sts).
Row 1: pattern to last 3 sts, p2tog tbl, p1.
Row 2: k1, ssk, patt to end.
Repeat these 2 rows until 16 (23, 28) sts remain
Continue until work is same length as back. Cast off for shoulder as for back.
Re-join yarn to other side of neck and complete to match, reversing shaping.

MAKING UP
Sew front to back along left shoulder seam.

NECKBAND
With right side of work facing and using 3.75 mm (size 5) needles, pick up and work 33 (35, 45) sts from back neck holder, 17 (21, 25) sts from left front neck edge, 21 (24, 25) sts from front neck holder and 17 (21, 25) sts from right front neck edge. Work 6 rows garter stitch and cast off loosely. Join right shoulder seam and neckband.

ARMBANDS (work 2)
With right side of work facing and using 3.75 mm (size 5) needles, pick up and knit 98 (114, 120) sts along armhole edge.
Work 6 rows Garter Stitch and cast off loosely. Join side seams using mattress stitch leaving 9 cm (3½ in) at hem for side slits.

Baby's log cabin blanket

By Tina Barrett

This subtle blanket design replicates in back-and-forth knitting the traditional pattern of a log cabin quilt in Blue-faced Leicester yarn.

The textured surface is created by using moss stitch for the logs, and stocking stitch for the lines dividing them. To get the pattern to work, you have to count a lot of rows (268 to be precise)! However, the end result is worth it!

Method

Place a stitch marker at the start of every wider 26-row panel.

Using 4 mm (size 6) needles, cast on 203 sts.
Row 1: Moss st 180 sts, k4, moss st 19 sts.
Row 2: Moss st 19 sts, p4, moss st 180 sts.
Repeat rows 1 and 2 for 26 rows.
Row 27: K184 sts, moss st 19 sts.
Row 28: Moss st 19 sts, p184 sts.
Row 29: As row 27
Row 30: As row 28
Row 31: Moss st 157 sts, k4, moss st 19 sts, k4, moss st 19 sts.
Row 32: Moss st 19 sts, p4, moss st 19 sts, p4, moss st 157 sts.
Repeat rows 31 and 32 for 26 rows.
Row 57: K161 sts, moss st 19 sts,

k4, moss st 19.
Row 58: Moss st 19, p4, moss st 19, p161.
Row 59: As row 57.
Row 60: As row 58.
Row 61: Moss st 19, k4, moss st 111, *k4, moss st 19* 3 times.
Row 62: *Moss st 19, p4* 3 times, moss st 111, p4, moss st 19.
Repeat rows 61 and 62 for 26 rows.

YARN REQUIREMENTS

Pure Blue-Faced Leicester DK yarn
• Total amount of wool by weight and approximate length
650g/1,430 m (1,547 yds)

Row 87: Moss st 19, k119, *Moss st 19, k4* twice, moss st 19.
Row 88: Moss st 19, *p4, moss st 19* twice, p119, moss st 19.
Row 89: As row 87.
Row 90: As row 88.
Row 91: *Moss st 19, k4* twice, moss st 65, *k4, moss st 19* 4 times.
Row 92: *Moss st 19, p4* 4 times, moss st 65, *p4, moss st 19* twice.
Repeat rows 91 and 92 for 26 rows.
Row 117: Moss st 19, k4, moss st 19, k73, *Moss st 19, k4* 3 times, moss st 19.
Row 118: Moss st 19, *p4, moss st 19* 3 times, p73, moss st 19, p4, moss st 19.
Row 119: As row 117.
Row 120: As row 118.
Row 121: *Moss st 19, k4* 8 times, moss st 19.
Row 122: Moss st 19, *p4, moss st 19* 8 times.
Repeat rows 121 and 122 for 26 rows.
Row 147: *Moss st 19, k4* 3 tImes, moss st 19, k50, *Moss st 19, k4* twice, moss st 19.
Row 148: Moss st 19, *p4, moss st 19* twice, p50, moss st 19, *p4, moss st 19* 3 times.
Row 149: As row 147.
Row 150: As row 148.
Row 151: *Moss st 19, k4* 4 times, moss st 42, *k4, moss st 19* 3 times.
Row 152: *Moss st 19, p4* 3 times, moss st 42, *p4, moss st 19* 4 times.
Repeat rows 151 and 152 for 26 rows.
Row 177: *Moss st 19, k4* twice, moss st 19, k96, moss st 19, k4, moss st 19
Row 178: Moss st 19, p4, moss st 19, p96, moss st 19, *p4, moss st 19* twice
Row 179: As row 177.
Row 180: As row 178.
Row 181: *Moss st 19, k4* 3 times, moss st 88, *k4, moss st 19* twice.
Row 182: *Moss st 19, p4* twice,

moss st 88, *p4, moss st 19* 3 times.
Repeat Rows 181 and 182 for 26 rows.
Row 207: Moss st 19, k4, moss st 19, k142, moss st 19.
Row 208: Moss st 19, p142, moss st 19, p4, moss st 19.
Row 209: As row 207.
Row 210: As row 208.
Row 211: *Moss st 19, k4* twice, moss st 134, k4, moss st 19.
Row 212: Moss st 19, p4, moss st 134, (p4, moss st 19) twIce.
Repeat rows 211 and 212 for 26 rows.
Row 237: Moss st 19, k184.
Row 238: P184, moss st 19.
Row 239: As row 237.
Row 240: As row 238.
Row 241: Moss st 19, k4, moss st 180.
Row 242: moss st 180, p4, moss st 19.
Repeat rows 241 and 242 for 26 rows.
Bind off in pattern.

FINISHING

Darn in loose yarn ends. Pin and block the blanket to shape. Add fringe to all edges: Cut lengths of yarn 30 cm (12 in) long. Take 3 or 4 strands, fold

MEASUREMENTS
Finished Size: 86 x 112 cm (34 x 44 in) without tassels

NEEDLES & NOTIONS
One pair 4 mm (size 6) needles
Stitch markers
Crochet hook for tassels

TENSION
24 sts x 26 rows = 10 cm (4 in) on 4 mm (size 6) needles and working in Log Cabin Pattern stitch.

ABBREVIATIONS (see also page 140)
Moss stitch on even number of stitches (repeat two rows):
Row 1: *k1, p1* repeat from * to * to end of row.
Row 2: *p1, k1* repeat from * to * to end of row.
Moss Stitch on an odd number of stitches (repeat one row):
Row 1: k1, *p1, k1* repeat from * to * to end of row.

in half, then, with RS of work facing, push crochet hook through edge of blanket. Catch hook on looped part of folded bundle and pull everything through the blanket edge. Pull yarn tails over top of right side edge, feed through looped eye of the bundle and pull tight to knot. Space evenly every 4–6 rows/sts.

DESIGNER PROFILE

Tina Barrett has designed knitwear for ten years. She loves working with natural pure wool, particularly for childrenswear. She has created designs for *Cornish Organic Wool*.

Castlemilk Moorit fleece

The Castlemilk was developed to provide decorative grounds management – a task it proved to do well and in a cost-effective manner. As a result of being specially created, it is among the rarest sheep in Britain. It survives thanks to farmers who are dedicated to keeping the breed alive.

The Castlemilk Moorit was 'invented' by Sir Jock Buchanan-Jardine to graze parkland on his estate at Castlemilk in Dumfriesshire, Scotland, in the early 20th century. He wanted brown sheep, so he crossbred brown (moorit) Shetland ewes with Manx Loagthan and wild Mouflon rams. The resulting rams have the show-off spiral horns of a Shetland (the ewes have outward-curved horns), while both rams and ewes have slight white markings from the Mouflon (these are typical of animals bred from relatively primitive origins). Their colour, small stature, short tail, and bare legs and heads, come from all three ancestors. As the name suggests, they are mid- or golden brown in colour. This is a really small sheep, with adult ewes weighing 35–40 kg (77–88 lbs) and rams only 50–55 kg (110–121 lbs).

When Sir Jock Buchanan-Jardine died in 1970, his flock was culled and dispersed, but one of today's rare breed heroes, Joe Henson, bought six ewes and a ram for his Cotswold Farm Park in Gloucestershire, UK. Thanks to this, and with the support of a few other buyers, the breed has survived.

Today it is popular with smallholders and crafters in the UK and there are also flocks in Belgium and the Netherlands. However, it remains among the rarest of British sheep. It is classified by the Rare Breeds Survival Trust as Vulnerable, with only around 900 registered breeding ewes.

BREED AT A GLANCE

Sheep type: Short-tailed.

Appearance: Short tails and horns in both ewes and rams; the ewes' horns curve outwards while the rams' sport show-off spirals. Mid-brown or golden-brown in colour with some slight camouflage white patches.

Rare breeds status: UK Rare Breeds Survival Trust classify it as Vulnerable.

Further information: UK breed society: www.castlemilkmoorit.co.uk.
Belgian breed society: www.castlemilkmoorit.be.

History: Developed by Sir Jock Buchanan-Jardine to graze the parkland on his estate at Castlemilk in Dumfriesshire in the early 20th century.

raw fleece

scoured fleece

carded fleece

FLEECE FACT FILE
Fleece weight: 1 kg (2–3 lb)
or less
Staple length: 5–7.5 cm (2–3 in)
or less
Micron count: 30–31.5 (up to 40)
Crimp: High
Handle: Medium
Natural colours: Light to
medium brown, tips usually
bleached cream by the sun
Mixed colours: None
Lustre: Semi-lustre

Close-up of knitted DK sample

DK with silk
and alpaca yarn

4-ply with silk
and alpaca yarn

Castlemilk Moorit yarn

The fleece of the Castlemilk Moorit has a wide range of fibre thickness from fine to coarse, probably due to the way it has been bred with other breeds to increase its numbers. Like many primitive breeds, if left to their own devices they will shed their fleeces rather than wait for shearing.

Although said to be soft, silky and fine, Castlemilk Moorit fleece is also often very short, and usually quite bitty. The crimp is relatively indistinct and fluffy, with the brown fibre bleached to cream at the tips by the sun and weather. With only rarely more than 1 kg (2.2 lbs) from each animal, it is too short to spin as a pure fibre commercially, although this can be done by hand (but it is best attempted by experienced handspinners).

There is little kemp, except in older animals on the back legs, and the fleece can be roo'd (combed or plucked out with the fingers) as an alternative to shearing. The yield on spinning short fleeces is much lower than for long fleeces, and Castlemilk Moorit is only suitable for woollen spinning, not worsted.

The sweater design included here uses my commercial yarn. I normally blend the Castlemilk Moorit fibres with 10% tussah silk and 10% alpaca of a similar colour: used alone the silk tends to swamp and overcome the fleece characteristics, and the alpaca helps to bring back the natural brown colour

As a Castlemilk Moorit fleece will not yield a lot of yarn, it may make sense to use it with wool from another breed. Here it has been combined with white Jacob yarn dyed red.

YARN USER'S GUIDE
Good for ...
- Weaving (suitable for weft only)
- Clothing
- Felting
- Blending (I find blending with silk and alpaca work well)

Not so good for ...
- Dyeing, although shades that combine with its natural colour are successful
- Weaving alone or where strength is needed

due to the additional bleaching effect of the pale cream of the silk. We make it in 4-ply and Double Knitting, but it might also work in thicker yarns spun as a pure version (note to self: try this sometime!).

By mixing young fleeces with silk and alpaca the wool can be worn next to the skin. If you would like to try other projects, this yarn is also suitable for anything made from Manx Loagthan, to which it is very similar, and also Black Welsh Mountain, Ryeland or Zwartbles.

Cable and rib sweater

by Sue Blacker and
Myra Mortlock

This pretty ribbed sweater offers a modern twist to classic cable designs, and the pattern includes plenty of options to enable you to personalise the fit and decoration.

The dramatic cable pattern on the front can be given a border of ribbing or moss or seed stitch; the ribs and cables can be twisted – or not – as desired. The ribbed sleeves include three lines of twisted rib.

The basic pattern is a one-size garment, which can be knitted as a cropped or as a longer length. The drop-shoulder, set-in sleeves reach the wrist, or can be lengthened to cover the hand or turned back to create a cosy cuff. If you prefer a shorter, bracelet sleeve, make them a few inches shorter. The high neck can be changed to a shorter turtleneck if you desire.

The sweater shown in the photographs was knitted on one size of needles throughout, and these are the instructions given in the pattern. However, for a firmer, stretchier rib at the hem, cuffs and neck, use needles a size smaller for these, and change to the larger size for the body and sleeves.

Further variations are given on pages 37 and 38.

YARN REQUIREMENTS

Castlemilk Moorit with alpaca and silk worsted-weight/DK yarn
• Total amount of wool by weight and approximate length
Cropped sweater: 500 g/1,100 m (1,119 yds)
Longer sweater: 650 g/1,430 m (1,547 yds)
• Add 50g/110 m (119 yds) for turtle neck if desired

Method

Tip: For a neat side edge, cast on extra 1 st at each end of the row and slip the first stitch and knit the last stitch of every row. (But remember to count them!)

Tip: Check the variations section (pages 38 and 39) as they may affect yarn required and start of back and front.

BACK (make 1)

With 4.5 mm (size 7) needles cast on 112 sts by cable cast on method.
Begin 3x2 rib pattern:
Row 1: K2 (p3, k2) repeat to end.
Row 2: (p2, k3) repeat to last 2 sts, p2.
Repeat until work measures 26 (40) cm (10 (16) in).

Shape underarm
Tip: To minimise the 'stepping' effect of shaping, slip through

MEASUREMENTS
Instructions are given for the cropped sweater first, followed by the longer version in brackets.
Garment size: chest 106 cm (42 in) when pressed.
Length from back neck to hem 43 (60) cm (17 (24) in).

NEEDLES & NOTIONS
1 pair 4.5 mm (size 7) needles
Cable needle
2 stitch holders or spare needles
Stitch markers (or waste yarn)

TENSION
Approx 21 sts x 22 rows = 10 cm (4 in) over 3x2 rib (RS: k2, p3, k2, p3 RS and WS: p2, k3) on 4.5 mm (size 7) needles
Adjust needle size to give required tension

ABBREVIATIONS (see also page 140)
P2togtbl: p2 sts together through the back of the loop (rather than the front).
T4L: (twist 4 sts to the left): slip next 3 sts onto cable needle and hold at front of work, p next st, then k3 from the cable needle.
T4R: (twist 4 sts to the right): place next st on to cable needle and hold at back of work, k3, then p1 from the cable needle.
C6F: slip next 3 sts onto cable needle, hold at front of work. K3, then k stitches from cable needle.
C6B: slip next 3 sts onto cable needle, hold at back of work. K3, then k stitches from cable needle.
TWL: k into the back of the 2nd st on left hand needle, then into the front of the 1st st, taking the 2 sts off together.
TWR: k into the front of the 2nd st on left hand needle, then into the front of the 1st st, taking off the 2 sts together.

back of the first stitch you are going to cast off.

Cast off 5 sts at start of next 2 rows, 3 sts at start of next 2 rows and 1 st at start of next 10 rows. 86 sts remain.
Continue without further shaping until work measures 43 (59) cm (17 (23) in) from cast on edge.

Shape the shoulders
Work 30 sts. Turn and work back along these 30 sts as follows: slip 1st stitch, k1, psso and work to end of row.
At shoulder edge cast off 9 sts, work to neck edge.
Repeat last 2 rows then dec once more at neck edge.

At shoulder edge cast off remaining sts.
Place centre 26 sts on a stitch holder.
Rejoin yarn to the remaining sts and complete the other side of the neck and shoulder, reversing the shaping.

FRONT (make 1)
The front features a central panel worked as follows: a central twisted cable panel of 26 sts on a reverse st st background of 6 sts at each side, making a total of 38 sts. The rib columns on either side of the panel may be twisted.
With 4.5 mm (size 7) needles cast on 112 sts.

Row 1: Work in 3x2 rib as for front for 37 sts. Set sts for centre panel: p6 for background (reverse stocking stitch), p1, T4L, T4R, p8, T4L, T4R, p1, p6 for background (reverse stocking stitch). Rib as before to end. Maintaining the rib and reverse st st background to the cable panel, work 36 rows of cable panel. Repeat until front measures 25 (40) cm (10 (16) in) from cast on edge.

Instructions for cable panel
Row 2: K2, p6, k10, p6, k2.
Row 3: P2, C6F, p10, C6F, p2.
Row 4: as row 2.
Row 5: P1, T4R, T4L, p8, T4R, T4L, p1.
Row 6: K1, p3, k2, p3, k8, p3, k2, p3, k1.
Row 7: T4R, p2, T4L, p6, T4R, p2, T4L.
Row 8: P3, k4, p3, k6, p3, k4, p3.
Row 9: K3, p4, T4L, p4, T4R, p4, k3.
Row 10: P3, k5, p3, k4, p3, k5, p3.
Row 11: T4L, p4, T4L, p2, T4R, p4, T4R.
Row 12: K1, p3, k5, p3, k2, p3, k5, p3, k1.
Row 13: P1, T4L. p4, T4L, T4R, p4, T4R, p1.
Row 14: K2, p3, k5, p6, k5, p3, k2.
Row 15: P2, T4L, p4, C6B, p4, T4R, p2.
Row 16: K3, p3, k4, p6, k4, p3, k3.
Row 17: P3, (T4L, p2, T4R) twice, p3.
Row 18: K4, p3, (k2, p3) 3 times, k4.
Row 19: P4, T4L, T4R, p2, T4L, T4R, p4 .
Row 20: K5, p6, k4, p6, k5.
Row 21: P5, C6F, p4, C6F, p5.
Row 22: as row 20.
Row 23: P4, T4R, T4L, p2, T4R, T4L, p4.
Row 24: as row 18.
Row 25: P3, (T4R, p2, T4L) twice, p3.
Row 26: as row 16.
Row 27: p2, T4R, p4, C6B, p4, T4L, p2.
Row 28: as row 14.
Row 29: P1, T4R, p4, T4R, T4L, p4, T4L, p1.

Row 30: as row 12.
Row 31: T4R, p4, T4R, p2, T4L, p4, T4L.
Row 32: as row 10.
Row 33: K3, p4, T4R, p4, T4L, p4, k3.
Row 34: as row 8.
Row 35: T4L, p2, T4R, p6, T4L, p2, T4R.
Row 36: as row 6.

Shape underarm as given for **back**. Continue in pattern until front measures 40 (56) cm (16.6 (22.5) in).

Neck shaping
Work 33 sts and turn.
Row 1: sl 1, k1, psso, work to end.
Row 2: work to last 2 sts, k2 tog. Repeat these 2 rows. 29 sts. Now decrease on right side rows only until 27 sts remain.

Shoulder shaping
Cast off 9 sts at armhole edge on next and following alternate row. Do not decrease at neck edge.
On next alternate row cast off remaining sts. Place central 20 sts on a holder.
Rejoin yarn to remaining sts and complete second shoulder, reversing shaping.

SLEEVES (make 2)

These instructions are for sleeves which end at the tip of the thumb without a turned-back cuff. To shorten the cuffs, reduce welt to 7 cm (3 in).

With 4.5 mm (size 7) needles cast on 52 sts.
Work 2x2 rib, twisting all rib lines on right side of work, using TWR for one sleeve and TWL for the other to make them symmetrical, for 12 cm (5 in), ending with right side row.
With wrong side facing, increase 1 st in all the knit stitch ribs to create 3x2 rib.
With right side facing, continue

in 3x2 rib but maintain twisted ribs in 3 centre rib lines only. Increase at both ends of next and every following 4th row until you have 102 sts. Periodically mark increase rows with stitch markers or thread for accurate joining.
Continue to knit without shaping until sleeve measures 53 cm (21 in) or desired length, from cast on edge.
Cast off 5 sts at the beginning of the next 4 rows.
Cast off remaining 82 sts.

MAKING UP

Join right shoulder. WS facing, pick up sts around neck *without knitting*: side of back neck 5 sts, stitch holder 26 sts, other side back neck 5 sts, side front neck 18 sts, front stitch holder 20 sts, side front neck 15 sts. (89 sts). RS facing, at front neck edge, knit and increase as follows: (K1 from needle, k1 from below next st, P2). Repeat 4 times. Work sts from holder in 2x2 rib. Increase in side neck as before to shoulder seam. Back neck (k1, k1 below st, p2) twice. Work 3x2 rib across sts from holder. Finish other side in same way.
Next row:, wrong side, work all sts as they present themselves.
Next row: Continue in 2x2 rib, twisting sts if desired.
Work 2.5 cm (1 in) in chosen pattern. Cast off loosely.
Join second shoulder, sew in sleeves, allow underarm body sides to wrap 2.5 cm (1 in) around sleeve top, and all other seams. Block.

VARIATIONS

For a more generous fit: work centre panel as given, but the remainder of front, back and sleeves in seed st or moss st with three-line rib panels at the centre of the sleeves and a five-line rib at centre of back of sweater.

TO KNIT SLEEVES FROM SHOULDER

With right sides together, sew one shoulder seam, matching rib lines. Open work out. Starting from the 3 st cast-off on body, mark sections as follows: 4 each on back and front with 10 sts to each section. Allow for 2 extra k sts at shoulder seam for centre line of sleeve.

Starting with 2 k sts, pick up and work 3x2 rib along 40 sts to shoulder, work 2 centre k sts then 40 sts in 3x2 rib to other armhole decrease, turn, cast on 5 sts. Work in pattern to row end. Repeat this row 3 more times. Continue to work down sleeve in 3x2 rib (with three twisted ribs at centre) without shaping for 6 rows.

Decrease at both ends of next and every 4th row until 66 sts remain. For precise joining, mark some decreases. Continue until work measures 40 cm (16 in).

To work the cuffs: With wrong side facing, k2tog in all 3st. ribs to give 2 by 2 rib. Right side facing, work twisted rib on knit sts across the whole row. Continue in twisted (2x2) rib for 12 cm (5 in). Cast off.

For a larger size: add 10 sts to front and back i.e. one 3x2 rib repeat on both sides of centre panel. Add 2 (2, 1) sts in that sequence to shoulder cast offs and 3 cm (1¼ in) to the length. The cropped version cannot be made any larger than this. The sleeve opening and sleeve should be made following the existing instructions. You will need an extra 50 g/110 m (119 yards) of yarn.

For a smaller size: use 3.75 mm (size 5) needles or reduce number of sts in front and back by 10 each per 20 cm (8 in) reduction (two 3x2 ribs to maintain symmetry).

For a turtle neck: work neck as given for 5 cm (2 in) in 2x2 rib, then change to 3x2 at fold over. Arrange ribs to match front (twist ribs if preferred). Work a further 8 cm (3 in), or more for a deep turtle neck. Allow an extra 50 g/110 m (119 yards) of yarn.

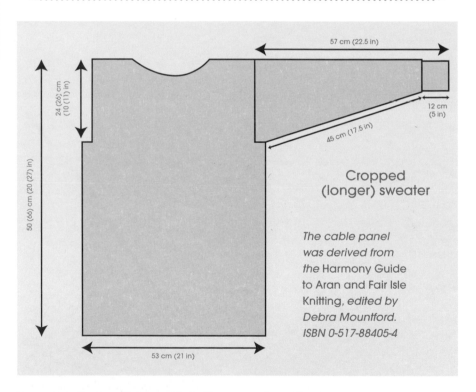

Cropped (longer) sweater

The cable panel was derived from the Harmony Guide to Aran and Fair Isle Knitting, *edited by Debra Mountford. ISBN 0-517-88405-4*

For a longer welt to match the cuffs: for back and front, cast on using a size smaller needles and work 3x2 or twisted rib for the first 14 cm (6 in). Change to 4.5 mm (size 7) needles and start cable pattern. Continue pattern above to underarm. If using twisted rib for the sleeve cuffs, either use twisted rib across the welts or use 3x2 rib for the back and sides of the front and twisted rib for the sts which will be below the cable on the front. You will need an extra 100 g/220 m (238 yards) of yarn. It may be best to buy extra as twisted rib can use more yarn.

Corriedale/Falklands fleece

Originally bred in New Zealand, the Corriedale is found all over the world, from Latin America to Australia and Europe, and can live on many types of terrain. Today, the majority are no longer pure-bred, and are likely to have proportions of Merino in them. They are sturdy, medium-sized sheep with bulky, fine fleeces.

Any description of these sheep is something of a history of British colonial sheep development: our 'Corriedale' is really generic Falklands wool, which is cross-bred and includes Polwarth, Merino, Coopworth and Corriedale genes.

As with the Castlemilk Moorit, Blue-faced Leicester and many more, the Corriedale owes its origin to some men with a mission – in this case James Little at the North Otago Station and William Soltau Davidson at Levels Station, on New Zealand's South Island. Between 1868 and 1874 both men concentrated on breeding sheep with consistently high quality fleeces. By the 1890s the Corriedale had become the country's first 'native' breed.

They can be large sheep, ranging from 60–80 kg (130–180 lbs) in ewes and from 79 kg up to even 125 kg (175-275 lbs) in rams. It is still a popular sheep in New Zealand and is also found in North and South America (it was first introduced to the US in 1914), Australia, and Eastern Europe as well as the Falkland Islands.

There are around 2.8 million Corriedales in New Zealand, although this is only 5–6 per cent of the total sheep population. However, you may struggle to find a true Corriedale due to the variations now available.

The fleece is known for its soft, finely crimped staples. It is versatile and makes an excellent hand-knitting yarn, as well as being woven to make medium-weight coats and jackets, worsteds and light tweeds.

BREED AT A GLANCE

Sheep type: Inbred crossbreed from Merino with Romney or Lincoln.

Appearance: Corriedales are medium-sized white sheep, with a thick fleece, no horns, a top-knot of wool on the head, wool on their legs, and black noses.

Rare breeds status: None.

Further information:
US breed society: www.americancorriedale.com.
Australian breed society: www.corriedale.org.au.

History: Originally developed in New Zealand, the Corriedale was the first of a family of breeds grown for their wool.

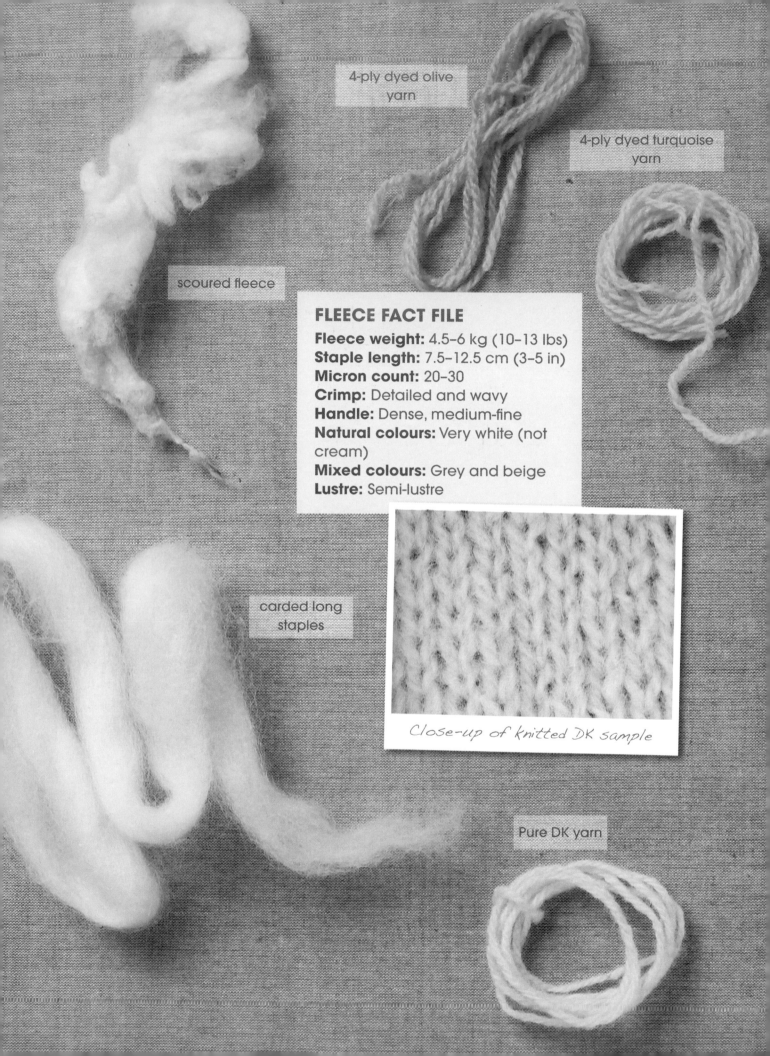

4-ply dyed olive
yarn

4-ply dyed turquoise
yarn

scoured fleece

FLEECE FACT FILE
Fleece weight: 4.5–6 kg (10–13 lbs)
Staple length: 7.5–12.5 cm (3–5 in)
Micron count: 20–30
Crimp: Detailed and wavy
Handle: Dense, medium-fine
Natural colours: Very white (not
cream)
Mixed colours: Grey and beige
Lustre: Semi-lustre

carded long
staples

Close-up of knitted DK sample

Pure DK yarn

Corriedale/Falklands yarn

If you want an easy-to-work-with, versatile, soft, semi-lustrous fleece, it is hard to beat Falkland Corriedale wool, which will cater for everything from baby clothes to rugs and afghans. The light bulkiness gives warmth and felts well.

Corriedale/Falklands wool is soft, very white and bulky, so that it makes yarns which seem fatter than others of the same specification – a 4-ply can knit up almost to resemble a DK yarn.

This wool is good for hand, worsted or woollen spinning, and felting. As it helps mohair hold together, we use ten per cent Corriedale in mohair knitting yarns. The fleece has a detailed, wavy crimp, which is distinct and not fluffy. However, you will find finer, coarser, longer and shorter Corriedale around the world.

The only drawback is that the fleece is so white that it almost appears (horror of horrors) as if it were synthetic when dyed! This is why we often blend it with a little fine Manx Loagthan, Black Welsh Mountain or Hebridean fleece to create

a more subtle colour. We have yet to find black and grey Corriedales. Because Corriedale is mainly farmed commercially in large flocks, any coloured lambs will be selected out very quickly.

For this soft, bulky yarn, we have created a design for a hot-water bottle cover. But you can use it for any of the Black Welsh Mountain, Castlemilk Moorit, Manx Loagthan, North Ronaldsay, Ryeland or Zwartbles designs in this book.

Pure Corriedale/Falklands yarn lends itself well to blending and dyeing. Its evenness, softness, and bulk makes it suitable for many craft projects. Use it to make knitted garments that are warm but not heavy to wear.

Corriedale hot-water bottle cover

By Sue Blacker

YARN REQUIREMENTS
Corriedale worsted-weight/DK yarn
• Total amount of wool by weight and length for a standard-sized hot-water bottle approximately 3 differently coloured 50 g/110 m (119 yds) balls (e.g. 1 purple, 1 pink and 1 grey or 1 turquoise, 1 blue and 1 grey, or 1 white, 1 grey, 1 fawn).

On a cold winter's night there's nothing better than curling up with a hot-water bottle with a cosy knitted cover. This design uses three colours of yarn to create narrow stripes each made up of two differently coloured yarns, while a combination of knit and purl stitches makes a stretchy rib pattern.

The cover is made to measure and so you need to measure your bottle and calculate the number of stitches you need to cast on. Instructions for this are given under Method.

By making narrow stripes there is no need to break and rejoin the yarn to create the pattern. Instead, you can just carry the spare colour up the side of the work. If you want to adapt the pattern to make wider stripes, you will need to sew or weave in the loose ends afterward to make things neat – use a large-eyed darning needle for this and weave in the ends along the edge of the knitting, so that each end is hidden in a stripe of the same colour. If you prefer to make a different pattern, remember that you need to have the same number of rows in each colour to use up all three balls evenly.

NEEDLES & NOTIONS
1 pair 6 mm (size 10)
needles

TENSION
Not necessary as this item
is made to measure.

ABBREVIATIONS
(see page 140)

Method

Measuring the bottle
Measure the hot water bottle,
or copy the dimensions of an
existing cover.

To calculate the width of the
knitting, measure the width of
your bottle and add 5cm (2 in).
For example, if the bottle is
25 cm (10 in) wide, your knitting
will be 30 cm (12 in) wide (25
cm plus 5 cm (10 in plus 2 in)).

Now calculate the overall
length of the cover. Measure the
length of the bottle, excluding
the neck and spout. You will
knit a piece of fabric this size to
make the first side, then bind/
cast off enough central stitches
to leave a gap for the neck,
and cast them on again in the
next row, to create a slit. The
second side needs to be long
enough to go around the base
of the bottle and come up
10 cm (4 in) on the other side
to enclose the bottle once you
have sewn it up. It will work like
the flap of a pillowcase, and
you can add buttons and loops
to it if you wish.

Cover (knit 1)

**For tips on colour knitting see
page 78.**
Using 6 mm (size 10) needles
and two colours of yarn
(colours A and B), cast on 7 sts
loosely for every 5 cm (2 in) of

your width measurement (e.g. if
the width is 20 cm (8 in), cast
on 28 sts; if 15 cm (6 in), then it
cast on 21 sts; if 25 cm (10 in),
35 sts, etc.).
**N.B. This pattern only works
with multiples of 4 stitches
plus 1**, so if necessary add
an extra stitch to make it work
(e.g. for 15 cm (6 in), you would
need 21 stitches, so there's no
need to add more, but for 28
and 35 stitches, make it 29 and
37, etc.).
Row 1: SL1, *k2, p2*, repeat
from * to * to last 4 sts, k2, p1, k1.
Work all following rows as Row
1, using tweed stripe pattern
and shaping as described
below.
Start in your first two colours (A
and B, whichever of the three
you prefer), work 2 rows, then
drop A and add in the third
colour, C. Knit 2 rows, then drop
B and add in A again. Work 2
rows. These six rows set the stripe
pattern: rows 1 and 2, A and B; 3
and 4, B and C; 5 and 6, C and
A and ensure that the ends and
balls of wool are always on the
same side of your work.
Continue stripe and rib pattern
until work is long enough to
cover the length of the hot-
water bottle plus a little easing
(an additional 2 rows).

Create an opening for the
neck of the bottle

Row 1: cast off the middle third
of stitches, continue to end.
Row 2: cast on middle third
stitches, continue to end.
Continue to work, maintaining
the stripe and rib pattern, until
the work will wrap around the
bottle. Knit a further 15 cm (6 in).
Cast off.

To make a collar for the neck
of the bottle
Using 6 mm (size 10) needles
and two colours of yarn pick
up and knit the stitches around
the neck slit. You can work each
side separately using standard
needles, or work in the round
with double-pointed or circular
needles.
Work the collar in k1, p1 rib,
maintaining the striped pattern.
Continue until the collar is twice
the length of the neck so that
it can be folded back. Bind/
cast off in rib and sew in the
ends securely. Sew up seams
if each side has been worked
separately.

MAKING UP

Fold the cover so that the
bottom flap is bent backwards
and stitch seams firmly. Turn it
inside so that the flap covers
the base of the hot-water bottle.
The rib pattern is the same on
both sides, so there is no right or
wrong side until it is sewn up.

Cotswold fleece

A big, old sheep! The Cotswold is said to be descended from animals brought to Britain by the Romans. It is certainly a long-standing resident. In medieval times it funded the imposing 'wool churches' of the Cotswolds area. Sadly, a great past has not heralded a great present, and it is now a rare breed.

The golden lanolin in the creamy lustrous wool, and the profits made from the fleeces, earned this imposing sheep the title of 'Cotswold Lion'. A truly beautiful lustre longwool, it should ideally be sheared twice a year to improve fleece quality.

The fleece is quite coarse in adults, and benefits from worsted spinning to soften it, but it does not contain any kemp. The staple length depends on whether it is shorn once or twice.

The Cotswold is not as tall as a Blue-faced Leicester but is considerably heavier, at up to 113–135 kg (250–275 lbs) in rams and 90–113 kg (200–250 lbs) in ewes. Their faces are slightly smiling, and their eyes are almost obscured when in full fleece with top-knot and fringe.

The US breed society states it was introduced to the US in 1832, and by 1879 it was the most popular breed in the country with over 760,000 recorded by 1914. It remained popular until the introduction of Merinos from Australia. By the 1980s there were fewer than 600 in the UK and US together.

Today, the Cotswold is designated as At Risk by the Rare Breeds Survival Trust, with less than 1,500 registered breeding ewes. The slow growing nature of this breed means that it is not seen as commercial for meat, while the wool, although long, thick and strong, has suffered with falling demand for carpets in recent years. Nevertheless, the efforts of rare breed enthusiasts have stablised the flock and it has a better outlook for the future.

BREED AT A GLANCE

Sheep type: Longwool.
Appearance: A big, broad and strongly built sheep without horns.
Rare breeds status: At Risk in the UK; Threatened in the US.
Further information:
UK breed society: www.cotswoldsheepsociety.co.uk.
US breed societies: www.cotswoldbreedersassociation. org, www.CotswoldSheep.us.com and www.cotswoldsheep.us.com/black_cotswolds.
History: Said to be descended from the sheep brought to Britain by the Romans, but may be earlier, and was the basis of the English medieval wool trade.

DK dyed guava
pink yarn

FLEECE FACT FILE
Fleece weight: 4–7 kg (9–15 lbs)
Staple length: 17.5–30 cm
(7–12 in)
Micron count: 34–40
Crimp: Wavy curls
Handle: Heavy and lustrous
Natural colours: Creamy white
Mixed colours: None
Lustre: High

natural DK
yarn

DK dyed
moss green
yarn

Close-up of natural DK sample

scoured fleece

raw fleece

carded fleece

Cotswold yarn

The creamy, lustrous wool of the Cotswold sheep is versatile, drapey and hard-wearing. It is also very strong – it can be used for socks and accessories as well as fine garments.

Cotswold wool is very hard-wearing and is ideal for carpets. Long, lustrous Cotswold wool was used to produce broadcloth and army uniforms (it felts well when woven to create a warm and water-resistant greatcoat).

Worsted-spun yarns are lean, shiny and creamy in their natural state, and bright when dyed thanks to the lustre, producing clear, vibrant colours.

Washed, individual locks of the fleece can be used for dolls' hair, Father Christmas beards, or they can be used in their natural state, or dyed, to decorate craft items.

The yarns are slightly fluffy, so a garment will gently felt over time to fill in the gaps between stitches. However, they are well suited to elegant, lacy and drapey styles, such as the cable pullover pattern shown here. Other good projects would include those used for Gotland yarns, socks, bags (particularly if made large and then felted), or yarns containing mohair. Or try it with a pattern designed for Blue-faced Leicester – you will get a good, but differently textured, result.

When in full fleece, the top knot and fringe can obscure the eyes of Cotswold sheep (right). The wool dyes well – here moss green and guava pink have been used (below).

YARN USER'S GUIDE

Good for ...
- Outerwear, accessories
- Felting
- Carpets
- Spinning and dyeing
- Garments requiring drape
- Hard-wearing garments

Not so good for ...
- Textured stitches
- Warmth and loft

Wavy cable jumper

By Amanda Jones

This attractive and feminine pullover, worked in the round in reverse stocking stitch, has a simple cable with a double wavy-lines design up the front and clever cables worked into the raglan shaping for the arm seams. It has a funnel neck and a small welt but no cuffs, and the ends of the sleeves curl inwards. It has a slightly gauzy texture to optimise the sheen and fineness of the worsted-spun Cotswold yarn.

Method

LOWER BODY
(make one)

Using 3.75 mm (size 5) circular needle cast on 198 (214:230:254) sts, being very careful not to twist the sts join into a ring and work pattern as follows.

Set up round
1st and 4th sizes only: K2 (-:-:1), (p5, k3) five (-:-:7) times, p5, k4, (p1, k4,(p5, k3) five (-:-:7) times, p5, k2 (-:-:1), place SM, k1 (-:-:2), (p5, k3) eleven (-:-:14) times to last sts: p5, k1 (-:-:2) place 2nd SM.

2nd and 3rd sizes only: P 0 (3:1:-), (k3, p5) 0 (6:7:-) times, k4, p1, j4, (p5, k3) 0 (6:7:-) times, p 0 (3:1:-), place SM, p – (2:4:-), (k3, p5) 0 (12:12:-) times to last sts: k3, p – (2:4:-), place 2nd SM.

All sizes
(Front section 103 (111:123:133), back section 95 (103:107:121) sts.)

YARN REQUIREMENTS

Pure Cotswold worsted-spun DK in natural or dyed shades
• Total amount of wool by weight and approximate length:
Small: 450 g/990 m (1,070 yds)
Medium: 500 g/1,100 m (1,190 yds)
Large: 550 g/1,210 m (1,309 yds)
Extra large: 600 g/1,320 m (1,428 yds)

MEASUREMENTS
Around the bust:
76-78 (86-92:96-101:106-112) cm
(30-32 (34-36:38-40:42-44) in)
Garment measurement: 84 (95:103:114) cm (33 (37.5:40.5:45) in)
Length to shoulder: 55(55:56:57) cm (21.5 (21.5:22:22.5) in)
Sleeve seam: 44 (44:45:46) cm (17.5 (17.5:17.75:18) in)

NEEDLES & NOTIONS
1 set 3.75 mm (size 5) circular needle 100 cm (40 in) long
1 set 3.25 mm (size 3) circular needle 80 cm (30 in) long
1 pair 3.75 mm (size 5) needles
Cable needle
4 stitch markers

TENSION
Approx 21sts and 32 rows = 10 cm (4 in) over st st on 3.75 mm
(size 5) needles.
Adjust needles to give required tension.

ABBREVIATIONS (see also page 140)
T4L: Twist 4 left: slip next 3 sts on to cable needle and hold at
the front of the work, purl next st then k 3 sts from cable needle.
T4R: Twist 4 right: slip next st on to cable needle and hold at
the back of the work, k next 3 sts then p st from cable needle.
C9F: Cable 9 front: slip next 4 sts on to cable needle and hold
at the front of the work, k4, p1, then k 4 sts from cable needle.
C4F: Cable 4 front: slip next 2 sts to cable needle and hold
at the front of the work, knit next 2 sts then k sts from cable
needle.
C4B: Cable 4 back: slip next to sts to cable needle and hold
at the back of the work, knit next 2 sts then k sts from cable
needle

DESIGNER PROFILE
Amanda Jones has designed knitwear since the late 1980s. She loves to use natural yarns as she feels that if you are investing your time in knitting something you should always use a yarn that will look good and last for more than one wash! She is inspired by nature and likes using textured stitches to create something interesting to knit.

1st round: Repeat set up round
2nd round: Rib as set for 31
(35:41:46) sts, (T4L, p4) twice, k4,
p1, k4, (p4, T4R) x 2, p4, Rib as
set to end.
This sets the position for the front
cable section.

Continue to work from round
2 of the chart reading all rows
from right to left until you have
completed 8 rounds.

Continue to work the cable
panel on reverse st st as set
from 9th round.
Repeat rounds 1–16 for the
pattern.

At the same time work side
decrease as follows:

Next round: (1st round WS
facing) *k1, k2tog tbl, pattern
to 3 sts before SM, k2tog, k1 to
SM; rep from * Decrease in this
way on the next 2 following 10th
rounds to make 97 (105:117:127)
sts between front stitch
markers and 86 (97:101:115) sts
between back stitch markers,
183 (202:218:242) sts in total.
Work 10 rounds in pattern
without shaping.

Next round: * k1, m1, pattern
to 1 st before next SM, m1, k1 to
SM; repeat from *.
Increase in this way on next
two following 20th rounds to
make 101 (109:121:131) sts for
front and 93 (101:105:119) sts for
back sections.

Continue without shaping until
the front measures 33 cm (13 in)
from beginning.
Next row: bind/cast off 6 (6:7:7)
sts, pattern to 6 (6:7:7) sts before
SM, cast off 12 (12:14:14), p to 6
(6:7:7) sts before next SM, bind/
cast off 6 (6:7:7) sts.

This leaves the Front section with
89 (97:107:117) sts and the Back
section with 81 (89:91:105) sts.
Break yarn and leave on a
holder.

LOWER SLEEVES
(make 2)
Using 3.75 mm (size 5) needles
cast on 61 (61:67:69) sts.
Begin with a knit row, working in
st st throughout work 20 rows.
Next row: decrease 1 st at
each end of this and the

KNITTER PROFILE

Jennie Martin enjoys knitting with the wide range of natural yarns – from lightwight to thick and chunky – that are available today, especially those using the natural colours of the fleece. She was taught to knit as a girl by her mother and grandmother. She especially enjoyed knitting and sewing for her children.

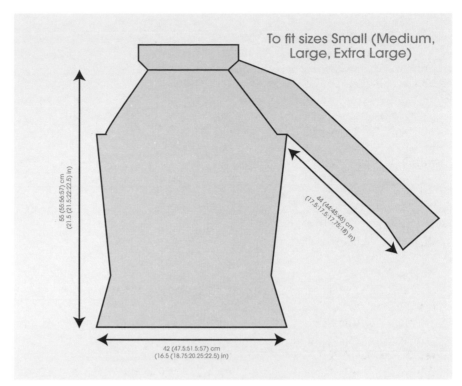

To fit sizes Small (Medium, Large, Extra Large)

55 (55:56:57) cm (21.5 (21.5:22:22.5) in)

44 (44:45:45:46) cm (17.5:17.5:17.75:18) in)

42 (47.5:51.5:57) cm (16.5 (18.75:20.25:22.5) in)

following 2 rows to make 55 (55:61:63) sts.
Work 9 rows straight then increase 1 st at each end of the following row and every following 6th row until there are 73 (87:91:95) sts.

For 1st size only: continue to increase on every following 8th row until there are 83sts.

All sizes: continue without shaping until the work measures 17.75, (17.75, 18, 18) in, 45 (45;46:46) cm from beginning of work, ending on a WS (knit) row.
Next row: cast off 6 (6:7:7) sts at the beginning of the next 2 rows, leaving 71 (75:77:81) sts. Break yarn and leave on a spare needle.
For 2nd sleeve do not break yarn.

Wavy pattern chart

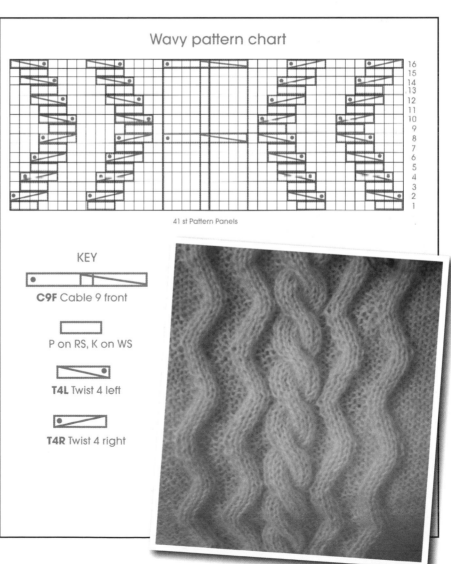

16
15
14
13
12
11
10
9
8
7
6
5
4
3
2
1

41 st Pattern Panels

KEY

C9F Cable 9 front

P on RS, K on WS

T4L Twist 4 left

T4R Twist 4 right

TOP SECTION
(worked in the round)

Joining round: with RS (purl) side of 2nd sleeve worked facing, k2, p to last 2 sts, k2 making 71 (75:77:81) sts, then with RS of body facing, starting with the front section, k2, continue in pattern as set work across front to last 2 sts, k2, being 89 (97:107:117) sts., then with RS (purl) side of sleeve facing, k2, p to last 2 sts k2 making 71 (75:77:81) sts. Finally, with RS of back section facing, k2, p to last 2 sts k2, making 81 (89:91:105) sts of back section and a total number of sts of 312 (336:352:384).

New placing of SM: Sl last 2sts (K sts) from the back section and place the SM here, now sl 2 sts back to LH needle.

Raglan shaping
Note: When counting the sts for each section, count between 4-st cable pattern at each end of section.

Next round: C4F, p2tog, p to 4 sts before end of sleeve section, p2tog tbl, C4B, p2tog, pattern across front section to last 4 sts, p2tog tbl, C4F, p2tog, p across sleeve section to last 4 sts, p2tog tbl, C4B, p2tog, p across back section to last 2 sts before SM, p2tog tbl.

Make cables and decrease either side of each cable in this way on every following 4th row and continue in pattern as set until 41 (43:45:49) sts remain on the sleeve sections, 59 (65:75:85) sts remain in front section and 51 (57:59:73) sts remain in back section. Work 3 more rounds so that the decrease round will be next.

Shape sleeve head
1st decrease row: C4F, p2tog, p 16 (17:18:20), p2tog, p1, p2tog tbl, p16 (17:18:20), p2tog tbl,

C4B, p2tog, pattern across front to last 2 sts before cable, p2tog tbl, C4F, p2tog, p16 (17:18:20), p2tog, p1, p2tog tbl, p16 (17:18:20), p2tog tbl, C4B, p2tog, p across back section, end p2tog tbl. Work 3 rounds straight for 2nd, 3rd and 4th SIZES, for 1st size only see below

For first size only: decrease 1st at each end of sleeve section only on every alternate round from now on as well as the 4th row decreases.

All sizes: 2nd decrease round: C4F, p2tog, p13 (15:16:18), p2tog, p1, p2tog tbl, p13 (15:16:18), p2tog tbl. C4B, pattern across front section to 2 sts before cable, p2tog tbl, work sleeve decrease and centre decrease as before, C4F, p2tog, p across back section to last 2 sts, p2tog tbl.

Decrease in the centre of the sleeve in this way on every following 4th round until 23 (43:37:33) sts remain on sleeve section.

4th size only: continue to decrease as before every 4th row to start of neck.

1st, 2nd and 3rd sizes only: now also decrease 1 st at each end of sleeve section on every following alternate row for 2nd and 3rd sizes, continuing with this for 1st size.

Continue to decrease 1 st either side of cables on front, back and central sleeve sections on every following 4th round as set until 13 (19;19;21) sts remain in sleeve section, 49 (53:63:71) sts in the front section and 41 (45:47:59) sts remain in back section for a total of 128 (148:160:184) sts. Work 2 rounds straight.

Neck
Change to 3.25 mm (size 3) circular needle.

Set up round for rib
1st size only: *k4, p2tog, (k3, p2) twice, k3, p2tog, k4*, p1, k3, p2tog, k3, p1, k3, p2tog, k3, (p1, k4) twice, p1, k3, p2tog, k3, p1, k3, p2tog, k3, p1; rep from * to *, p1, k3, p2tog, (k3, p1) six times, p2tog, k3, p1 making 118 sts
2nd size only: * k4, (p1, k3) x 4, p1, k4*, p1, k3, p2tog, (k3, p1) x 2, k3, p2tog, k3, (p1, k4) x 2, p1, k3, p2tog, (k3, p1) x 2, k3, p2tog, k3, p1; rep from * to *, p1, k3, p2tog, (k3, p1) x 8, k3, p2tog, k3, p1 making 142 sts.
3rd size only: *k4, p1, k3, p2tog, k3, p1, k3, p2tog, k3, p1, k4*, p1, k3, p2tog, (k3, p1)x 3, k3, p2tog, k3, p1, (k4,p1)x2, k3, p2tog, (k3, p1) x3, k3, p2tog, k3, p1; rep from * to *, p1, k3, p2tog, (k3, p1) x 8, k3, p2tog, k3, p1 making 150 sts.
4th size only:* k4, p1, k3, (p2tog, k3)x3, k3, p2tog, k4*, p1, k3, p2tog, (k3, p1)x4, k3, p2tog, k3, (p1, k4)x2, p1, k3, p2tog, (k3, p1) x4, k3, p2tog, k3, p1; rep from * to *, p1, k3, p2tog, (k3, p1)x2, k3, (p2tog, k3, p1, k3)x4, p2tog, k3, p1 making 166 sts.
Continue in rib and cables as set until the rib measures 2.25ins, 6cms from beginning.
Cast off in rib.

TO FINISH

Sew in all loose ends. Join sleeve seam. Sew cast off edge of sleeve to the cast off edge of the front and back under the arms.
Press lightly.

Galway fleece

The Galway sheep is now considered to be the only 'native' Irish sheep. It is difficult to be sure that any sheep is a native anymore! The result of selective breeding between Irish breeds and English Leicesters, it took over after the disappearance of its close relative the Roscommon early in the 20th century, reaching a third of the Irish flock by 1965. Despite this, it is rare today.

Although it is classified as a 'longwool' sheep, the staples from a Galway fleece are not exceptionally long and do not have the lustre of other longwools; they are firm and crisp with an indistinct, fluffy crimp. Some fleeces can be used for garments worn next to the skin; others are suitable for sweaters and jackets. The fleece is all-white.

The Galway has a characteristic short neck, so that the head appears to be an extension of the long, straight back. The sheep are hornless, with a top-knot, and wool down to the knees. They are similar in appearance to the Romney, particularly around the head and ears.

The adult sheep are medium-sized, with the ewes weighing around 74 kg (163 lbs) and the rams 80 kg (176 lbs) on average. Galway ewes are long-lived, lambing successfully up to the age of ten and, with good husbandry, are able to produce and rear twins.

Most Galways are farmed in Ireland. Due to competition from imported breeds, the number of registered ewes fell from around 700 in 37 flocks in 1965, to only just over 100 in 10 flocks by 1993. But this is now recovering and there were nearly 870 sheep in 40 flocks by 2007. This would qualify the breed for Vulnerable status under the UK's Rare Breeds Survival Trust criteria. It has gained the Galway breed recognition and protection at national level as part of the country's Rural Environment Protection Scheme.

There are a few flocks in the UK but none are reported in the US.

BREED AT A GLANCE

Sheep type: Longwool.
Appearance: White and hornless.
Rare breeds status: Listed as Vulnerable in Ireland, a conservation breed in the US, on the UK Rare Breeds Survival Trust watchlist.
Further information: Irish breed society: www.galwaysheep.ie. Galway Sheep Breeders Society of Great Britain: www.sheep.ukf.net.
History: A variant of the now extinct Roscommon breed which it succeeded thanks to it being faster growing (and therefore more commercial), finer and heavier.

clean fleece

Aran yarn

FLEECE FACT FILE
Fleece weight: 2.5–3.5 kg (5.5–7.7 lbs)
Staple length: 11.5–14 cm (4.5–5.5 in)
Micron count: Around 30-plus
Crimp: Indistinct wavy
Handle: Crisp
Natural colours: True white (not cream)
Mixed colours: None
Lustre: None

Close-up of white Aran knitted sample

raw fleece

carded fleece

Galway yarn

The clean, white Galway is a great, do-it-all fibre. It crosses the boundaries between lustrous longwools and mid-range or Downland wools. In general it makes softer yarns than the wool produced by the more numerous Lleyn, with good definition. It deserves to be more widely used.

The fleece of the Galway sheep is of a medium length, with a soft, fluffy and indistinct crimp. The staples are long enough for worsted spinning.

Worsted-spun Galway yarn gives good stitch definition when knitted, and so Galway yarn is a good candidate for textured knits such as Guernseys. It is also ideal for traditional Aran-style textured pullovers. The Aran Islands are off the coast of Ireland, in the Galway Bay, and so the knitting developed there would surely be related to the native fleeces!

The wool is mid-range in fineness, nor is it the softest available (although some fleeces yield wool soft enough to be worn next to the skin), but it is hard-wearing. It does not felt well. Thus, the stitches in a textured pattern remain distinct after years of wear. When dyed, Galway wool has a clear, strong colour.

I have chosen a modern take on an Aran sweater design for this Galway pattern. Other options would include the patterns in Gotland or Cotswold yarn, which will have a more textured result. You could also try the Jacob, North Ronaldsay, Ryeland and Zwartbles patterns, or the bag in Hebridean yarn.

When knitted, Galway yarn gives great stitch definition in cable designs as well as between knit and purl stitches – adding texture to the simplest knitted fabric.

Pucker cable tunic

By Amanda Crawford

This attractive all-over cable tunic has a puckered cable design created by cabling on fewer, and then more, stitches in the cable panels. It has drop shoulders and hangs straight from the shoulders. The relaxed feel is enhanced by the turned-back ribbed cuffs and a grown-on funnel neck – a simple rib roll-neck may be substituted to match the cuffs, if desired. It is ideal for a 'big' look, and pairs well with leggings and boots, or when worn casually with jeans. It can also be made longer to create a tunic dress, or adapted, using either neck design, with a rib welt and shorter cuffs for a man's outdoor pullover.

DESIGNER PROFILE

Amanda Crawford works almost exclusively with natural wool. She designed knitwear for major stores before deciding to follow her passion for hand-knitting. Today she designs for magazines.

YARN REQUIREMENTS

Pure Galway Wool Aran yarn
• Total amount of wool by weight and approximate length
UK size 8: 900 g / 1,260 m (1,368 yds)
UK size 10: 900 g / 1,260 m (1,368 yds)
UK size 12: 1,000 g / 1,400 m (1,520 yds)
UK size 14: 1,000 g / 1,400 m (1,520 yds)
UK size 16: 1,100 g / 1,540 m (1,672 yds)
UK size 18: 1,100 g / 1,540 m (1,672 yds)
UK size 20: 1,200 g / 1,680 m (1,824 yds)
UK size 22: 1,200 g / 1,680 m (1,824 yds)

Method

BACK and FRONT
(make two, both alike)

Using 5 mm (size 8) needles cast on 105 (109, 115, 121, 129, 135, 141, 145) sts.

Foundation rows:
UK Sizes 8, 10, 12, 14 and 22
Row A (RS): p2 (4, 7, 10, -, -, -, 1), *k8, sl 1, k8, p4, rep from * to last 19 (21, 24, 27, -, -, -, 18) sts, k8, sl 1, k8, p2 (4, 7, 10, -, -, -, 1).
Row B: k2 (4, 7, 10, -, -, -, 1), *p17, k4, rep from * to last 19 (21, 24, 27, -, -, -, 18) sts, p17, k2 (4, 7, 10, -, -, -, 1).

UK Sizes 16, 18 and 20
Row A (RS): P- (-, -, -, 1, 4, 7, -), sl 1, k8, p4, *k8, sl 1, k8, p4, rep from * to last - (-, -, -, 10, 13, 16, -) sts, k8, sl 1, P- (-, -, -, 1, 4, 7, -).
Row B: K- (-, -, -, 1, 4, 7, -), p9, k4, *p17, k4, rep from * to last - (-, -, -, 10, 13, 16, -) sts, p9, k- (-, -, -, 1, 4, 7, -).

Continue in pattern:
UK Sizes 8, 10, 12, 14 and 22
Row 1 (RS): P2 (4, 7, 10, -, -, -, 1), *k8, sl 1, k8, p4, rep from * to last 19 (21, 24, 27, -, -, -, 18) sts, k8, sl 1, k8, p2 (4, 7, 10, -, -, -, 1).
Row 2 and all alternate rows:- K2 (4, 7, 10, -, -, -, 1), *p17, K4, rep from * to last 19 (21, 24, 27, -, -, -, 18) sts, p17, k2 (4, 7, 10, -, -, -, 1).
Row 3 (RS): As row 1.
Row 5 (RS): P2 (4, 7, 10, -, -, -, 1), *CB8, sl 1, CF8, p4, rep from * to last 19 (21, 24, 27, -, -, -, 18) sts, k8, sl 1, k8, p2 (4, 7, 10, -, -, -, 1).
Row 7 (RS): As row 1.
Row 9 (RS): P2 (4, 7, 10, -, -, -, 1), *k2, CB6, sl 1, CF6, k2, p4, rep from * to last 19 (21, 24, 27, -, -, -, 18) sts, k2, CB6, sl 1, CB6, k2, p2 (4, 7, 10, -, -, -, 1).
Row 11 (RS): As row 1.
Row 13 (RS): P2 (4, 7, 10, -, -, -, 1), *k4, CB4, sl 1, CF4, k4, p4, rep from * to last 19 (21, 24, 27, -, -, -, 18) sts, k4, CB4, sl 1, CB4, K4, p2 (4, 7, 10, -, -, -, 1).

MEASUREMENTS
Bust size: 82 (86, 90, 96, 102, 107, 112, 117) cm (32 (34, 36, 38, 40, 42, 44, 46) in)
Garment size: 92 (96, 100, 106, 112, 118, 122, 126) cm (36.5 (38, 39.5, 42, 44, 46, 48, 49.5) in)
Length: 55 (55, 58, 58, 61, 61, 64, 64) cm (21.5 (21.5, 23, 23, 24, 24, 25, 25) in)
Instructions are given for the smallest size first, followed by the larger sizes in brackets.

NEEDLES & NOTIONS
A pair needles 5 mm (size 8)
A pair 5 mm (size 8) circular needles
Cable needle

TENSION
Approx 23 sts x 25.5 rows = 10 cm (4 in) over cable pattern on 5 mm (size 8) needles
Adjust needle size to give required tension

ABBREVIATIONS (see also page 140)
CB8 (6, 4) = slip next 4 (3, 2) sts on to a cable needle and hold at back of work. K next 4 (3, 2) sts then k sts from cable needle.
CF8 (6, 4) = slip next 4 (3, 2) sts on to a cable needle and hold at front of work. K next 4 (3, 2) sts then k sts from cable needle.
Sl 1 = slip one stitch with yarn held at back of work (including after purl stitches)

SKILL LEVEL

Row 14: As row 2.
These 14 rows set pattern. Continue straight in pattern until work measures 21 (21, 22, 22, -, -, -, 24.5) in (53 (53, 56, 56, -, -, -, 62) cm), ending with RS facing.

Continue in pattern:
UK Sizes 16, 18 and 20
Row 1 (RS): P- (-, -, -, 1, 4, 7, -), sl 1, k8, p4, *k8, sl 1, k8, p4, rep from * to last - (-, -, -, 10, 13, 16, -) sts, k8, sl 1, P- (-, -, -, 1, 4, 7, -).
Row 2 and all alternate rows: K- (-, -, -, 1, 4, 7, -), p9, k4, *p17, k4, repeat from * to last -(-, -, -, 10, 13, 16, -) sts, p9, k- (-, -, -, 1, 4, 7, -).
Row 3 (RS): As row 1.
Row 5 (RS): P- (-, -, -, 1, 4, 7, -), sl 1, CF8, p4, *CB8, sl 1, CF8, p4, rep from * to last - (-, -, -, 10, 13, 16, -) sts, CB8, sl 1, p-(-, -, -, 1, 4, 7, -).
Row 7 (RS): As row 1.
Row 9 (RS): P- (-, -, -, 1, 4, 7, -), sl 1, k2, CF6, p4, *k2, CB6, sl 1, CF6, k2, p4, rep from * to last - (-, -, -,

10, 13, 16, -) sts, k2, CB6, sl 1, p- (-, -, -, 1, 4, 7, -).
Row 11 (RS): As row 1.
Row 13 (RS): P- (-, -, -, 1, 4, 7, -), sl

1, k4, CF4, p4, *k4, CB4, sl 1, CF4, k4, p4, rep from * to last -(-, -, -, 10, 13, 16, -) sts, k4, CB4, sl 1, p- (-, -, -, 1, 4, 7, -).

Row 14: As row 2.

These 14 rows set pattern, continue straight in pattern until work measures - (-, -, -, 59, 59, 62, -) cm (- (-, -, -, 23¼, 23¼, 24½, -) in), ending with RS facing.

Shape Shoulders
All sizes

Keeping pattern correct, bind/cast off 10 (11, 11, 12, 13, 14, 15, 16) sts at beginning of next 2 rows, 10 (10, 11, 12, 13, 14, 15, 15) sts at beginning of following 2 rows and 9 (10, 11, 12, 13, 14, 14, 15) sts at beginning of next 2 rows, leaving 47 (47, 49, 49, 51, 51, 53, 53) sts.

Leave remaining 47 (47, 49, 49, 51, 51, 53, 53) sts on a stitch holder.

SLEEVES
(make two)

Using 5 mm (size 8) needles cast on 74 (74, 79, 79, 84, 84, 84, 84) sts.

Row 1: (RS): P3 *k3, p2, rep from * to last 6 sts, k3, p3.

Row 2: K3 *p3, k2, rep from * to

last 6 sts, p3, k3.

These 2 rows set rib, continue straight in rib for 20 cm (8 in) ending with WS row facing for next row. Repeat row 2, increasing 3 (3, 2, 2, 3, 3, 3, 3) sts evenly across row. 77 (77, 81, 81, 87, 87, 87, 87) sts.

Cont in pattern:

Row 1 (RS): p2, K3 (3, 5, 5, 8, 8, 8, 8), p4 *k8, sl 1, k8, p4, rep from * to last 5 (5, 7, 7, 10, 10, 10, 10) sts, K3 (3, 5, 5, 8, 8, 8, 8), p2.

Row 2 and every following alternate row: k2, P3 (3, 5, 5, 8, 8, 8, 8), K4, *p17, k4, repeat from * to last 5 (5, 7, 7, 10, 10, 10, 10) sts, p3 (3, 5, 5, 8, 8, 8, 8), k2.

Continue with rows 3-14 in pucker cable pattern as placed, increasing 1st each end of next row and every following 4th row 2 sts in from edge and taking extra sts into pattern until 109 (109, 115, 115, 121, 121, 127, 127) sts.

P first and last 2 sts to give a neat edge for sewing up.

Continue straight in pattern until sleeve measures 19.5 (19.5, 19.5, 19.5, 20.5, 20.5, 21.25, 21.25) in (50 (50, 50, 50, 52, 52, 54, 54) cm) ending with RS facing for next row.

Bind/Cast off.

FINISHING

Press work carefully. Join shoulder seams.

NECK TRIM

Using 5 mm (size 8) circular needle transfer sts from stitch holders. 94 (94, 98, 98, 102, 102, 106, 106) sts.

Keeping pattern as set continue straight for 8cm (3 in), or longer if desired, ending with RS facing for next row. Bind/Cast off.

Sew side seams and underarm together as one continuous seam, remembering to reverse the seam for the first 12 cm (4.75 in) of the cuff as this will be turned back.

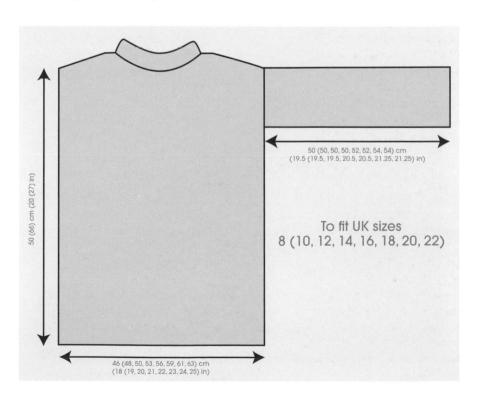

50 (50, 50, 50, 52, 52, 54, 54) cm
(19.5 (19.5, 19.5, 20.5, 20.5, 21.25, 21.25) in)

50 (66) cm (20 (27) in)

46 (48, 50, 53, 56, 59, 61, 63) cm
(18 (19, 20, 21, 22, 23, 24, 25) in)

To fit UK sizes
8 (10, 12, 14, 16, 18, 20, 22)

Gotland fleece

As a Gotland owner of many years I am biased – I consider this to be an extremely intelligent sheep, with a sense of humour and mischief. Today's Gotland is an improved version of the original breed, with a more consistent fleece and conformation. Although they no longer have horns, they have distinct horn craters, and some develop mini vestigial horns or scurs.

The longwool fleece of the Gotland sheep is soft enough to be worn next to the skin. The texture is so light it can be similar to that of a fine mohair.

The characteristics of an individual fleece will depend on the strain of the breed, but they are always long, lustrous and with a wavy – even curly – crimp.

Gotlands, particularly the rams, may have a dark mane of coarse hair at the neck. The lambs are born black, and this colour remains on the hairless legs and heads. The skin is naturally grey in colour, but some sheep have one or more white socks, white around the eyes, or white blazes on the face.

The Gotland is sometimes known as the three-crop sheep as it is good for fleece, skins and meat. It was first imported into the UK in the 1970s, and to the US in 2003. It is also farmed in Australia, Sweden, Holland and Denmark.

The adult sheep are small, the ewes growing to 55–70 kg (121–154 lbs) and the rams to 75–85 kg (165–187 lbs). Like other primitive sheep breeds they are hardy animals. Although not numerous in the UK, with around 200 registered breeding ewes, they are becoming increasingly popular.

In New Zealand, the famous Stansborough flock produced the wool used for the cloaks worn by the Hobbits in *The Lord of the Rings* films.

BREED AT A GLANCE

Sheep type: Primitive, northern short-tailed.
Appearance: Grey – sometimes with white markings – black heads, and legs; no horns.
Rare breeds status: None.
Further information: UK breed society: www.gotlandsheep.com.
North American and US breed societies: www.americangotlandsheep.com and www.gsbana.org.
History: From the island of Gotland, off the coast of Sweden, where they were known as gute sheep. The breed was originally developed for its skin; this may have begun in the time of the Vikings.

dark grey
4-ply yarn

dark grey DK
yarn

dark grey denim
over-dyed DK yarn

mid-grey slate over-
dyed 4-ply yarn

FLEECE FACT FILE
Fleece weight: 1–4 kg (2–8 lbs)
Staple length: 25 cm (10 in)
Micron count: 28–32, but can be well
below this for lambs and selected
adults, as low as 20 in some cases
Crimp: Well developed and wavy
Handle: Soft and supple
Natural colours: Shades of grey
(from pale to charcoal); some white
and brown
Mixed colours: Greys and brownish grey
Lustre: High

raw fleece

carded mid-grey fleece

carded pale
fleece

Close-up of dark grey DK knitted sample

mid-grey DK yarn

scoured
fleece

carded dark-grey
fleece

pale DK yarn

Gotland yarn

Gotland wool is very soft and fine, with various shades of grey from silver to charcoal. Among sheep, Gotlands probably produce a fleece most like mohair in texture. It has a distinct lock formation, with a neat, tiny crimp in lambs, which lengthens out into wavy ringlets as they grow older.

Make the most of the many shades of wool available from a Gotland fleece to create naturally multicoloured garments. The result will be a soft, silky garment that drapes well.

As a lustre longwool, Gotland dyes wonderfully, and the over-dyeing of the natural silvers and greys produces very attractive shades, particularly when using pinks, blues and purples, but also in greens, rusts and golds.

Although Gotland wool can be worsted-spun to enhance its lustre, it may then shed or pill as the smooth hairs gently work their way free of the yarn. As a result it is better semi-worsted or woollen-spun, which results in a lean, stylish but slightly fluffy yarn. Hand-spinners will find Gotland quite a challenging task.

Gotland may sometimes feel hard when newly spun as it responds less well to twisting than some fibres, but it softens beautifully with age.

Gotland can be spun fine for lace work or thick for chunky sweaters, but the propensity to felt will mean that over time a textured Aran or Guernsey design will gradually lose its crisply distinct details, although it will also become warmer and more windproof.

Gotland yarn can happily be used as a substitute to knit the patterns designed for Cotswold and Wensleydale yarns in this book. It can also be used for the patterns designed for Jacob wool, or the Shetland lacy scarf, where it will achieve a different, more draped style.

The fleece will grow up to 30 cm (12 in), but farmers rarely allow this because it felts very easily and, if left on the animal for a year, the beautiful individual locks will become matted and impossible to separate for spinning (although the matted fleece makes an ideal pet bed or home insulation). To prevent this Gotlands are shorn twice a year to produce fleece with a staple length of 10–15 cm (4–6 in). Like most sheep and goats, Gotlands can produce coarser wool with age, including straighter hairs, kemp and less crimp.

Long cardigan with hand-warmer pockets

By Myra Mortlock and Sue Blacker

This cardigan has a deep welt, which can be left unsewn with side slits for a more relaxed fit or sewn together. Using 4.5 mm (size 7) needles for the whole body will leave the welt looser, which is probably more flattering for this length, but we suggest you use 4 mm (size 6) or even 3.75 mm (size 5) needles for the collar to make it stiffer. The buttons are optional. The deep shawl collar can be made in one colour or with a contrast lining. A multi-cable motif decorates the centre-back. Hand-warmer pockets add extra warmth.

The sleeves are worked downwards with two options: either a tight, long cuff in two and two rib to match the front bands (worked on 4 mm (size 6) needles) or doubled offset rib cuffs to match the collar and which make the garment suitable to wear as a jacket or coat. If making the tight cuff, the sleeves can be worked on circular and double-pointed needles; the offset rib version works best on two needles.

We have used Gotland DK yarn, but any other DK yarn would be suitable.

YARN REQUIREMENTS

Gotland worsted-weight Double Knitting yarn
• Total amount of wool by weight and approximate length:
Small: 750 g/1,650 m (1,785 yds)
Medium: 800 g/1,760 m (1,904 yds)
Large: 850 g/1,870 m (2,023 yds)

Method

BACK (make one)

Using 4 mm (size 6) needles (or 4.5 mm (size 7) for looser welt), cast on 109 (117, 125) sts.
Row 1: K2, p2 to last st, k1.
Row 2: as row 1.
Repeat until work measures 6 in (15 cm) for all sizes.
Change to 4.5 mm (size 7) needles and knit one row, increasing 1 st in centre of row to give 110 (118, 126) sts.
Continue in stocking stitch until work measures 58 cm (23 in) from cast-on edge.

Shape armhole
Tip: to get a smooth curve, slip the first st in all these cast off rows.
Cast off 5 sts at start of next 2 rows, 4 sts at start of following 2 rows, 3 sts next 2 rows, 2 sts following 2 rows and 1 st next 2 rows. Total decrease 15 sts on each side.

Centre motif in 3 sections
Section 1:
RS facing, mark centre 34 sts for cable motif (30 sts with border of 2 reverse stocking st each side).
Begin pattern as follows:
RS facing, k 23 (27, 31) sts, p2, T3, p2, T3, p2, T3, p4, T3, p2, T3, p2, T3, p2, K to end.

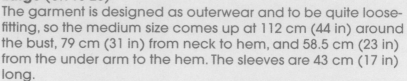
Size Small (UK 10-12)
Medium (UK 14 -16)
Large (UK 18-20)
The garment is designed as outerwear and to be quite loose-fitting, so the medium size comes up at 112 cm (44 in) around the bust, 79 cm (31 in) from neck to hem, and 58.5 cm (23 in) from the under arm to the hem. The sleeves are 43 cm (17 in) long.
NOTE: to shorten cardigan, reduce length of body by 2.5 cm (1 in) below and above the pockets. To re-size it to make it slightly smaller or larger, use one size smaller or larger needles. Instructions are given for the smallest size first, followed by medium and large in brackets

SKILL LEVEL

NEEDLES & NOTIONS
One pair each of needles 3.75 mm (size 5), 4 mm (size 6) and 4.5 mm (size 7)
Stitch markers or coloured thread
Stitch holder
7 buttons (optional)

TENSION
Approx 21 sts x 22 rows = 10 cm (4 in) over stocking stitch on 4.5 mm (size 7) needles
Adjust needle size to give required tension.

ABBREVIATIONS (see also page 140)
Offset 2 x 2 rib: (see instructions below, k2, p2 all rows).
2 x 2 rib (for front bands): Row 1: (k2, p2) repeat to end. Row 2: (p2, k2) repeat to end.
T3 (twist 3): slip next 2 sts onto cable needle and hold at back of work, knit next st then knit 2 sts from cable needle.
T5L (twist 5 left): slip next 3 sts onto cable needle and hold at front of work, purl next 2 sts from left-hand needle, then knit sts from cable needle.
T5R (twist 5 right): slip next 2 sts onto cable needle and hold at back of work, knit next 3 sts from left-hand needle, then purl sts from cable needle.
C6F (cable 6 front): slip next 3 sts onto cable needle and hold at front of work, knit next 3 sts from left-hand needle, then knit sts from cable needle.
C6B (cable 6 back): slip next 3 sts onto cable needle and hold at back of work, knit next 3 sts from left-hand needle, then knit sts from cable needle.

Next row: work all sts as they present themselves.
Continue, repeating these 2 rows until 14 rows of pattern have been worked.

Section 2:
Work cable design over 14 rows as follows:

Row 1: K 23 (27, 31) p2 (T5L) 3 times. (T5R) 3 times p2, k 23 (27, 31).
Row 2: P 23 (27, 31) k4, p3, k2, p3, k2, p6, k2, p3, k2, p3, k4, p23 (27, 31).
Row 3: K 23 (27, 31) p4, (T5L) twice, C6B, (T5R) twice, p4, k to end.

Row 4: P 23 (27, 31) k6, p3, k2, p12, k2, p3, k6, p to end. Instructions following are for the centre panel of 34 sts only.

Row 5: P6, T5L, (C6F) twice, T5R, p6.

Row 6: K8, p18, k8.

Row 7: P8, (C6B) 3 times, p8.

Row 8: K8, p18, k8.

Row 9: P6, T5R, (C6F) twice, T5L, p6.

Row 10: as row 4.

Row 11: P4, (T5R) twice, C6B, (T5L) twice, p4.

Row 12: as row 2.

Row 13: P2, (T5R) 3 times (T5L) 3 times, p2.

Row 14: K2, (p3, k2) twice, p3, k4, p3, (k2, p3) twice, k2.

Section 3:

Repeat section 1 working 13 rows. End with RS row.
Work 9 (11, 13) rows stocking stitch to shoulder.

Shape shoulder

RS facing, knit 28 (32, 36) sts and turn. Leave remaining sts on hold (they can stay on needle).

Row 1: at neck edge, slip 1 purlwise, p1, psso purl to end.

Row 2: knit without shaping. Repeat row 1.
At shoulder edge, cast off 8 (9, 10) sts.
At neck edge, slip 1 purlwise, p1, psso as before.
Repeat these 2 rows.
Decrease once more at neck edge then cast off all remaining shoulder sts.
Leaving 24 (24, 24) sts on holder for back of neck, make second shoulder reversing all shaping.

RIGHT FRONT
(make one)

Using 4 mm (size 6) needles (or 4.5 mm (size 7) for looser welt), cast on 55 (59, 63) sts.
Work in offset 2x2 rib, K2, P2 to last 3 sts, K2, P1 to same length as back.
Change to 4.5 mm (size 7) needles and st st and work 24 rows.
Divide for pocket opening.
RS facing, k 30 sts and turn,

leaving remaining 29 sts on hold. WS facing, cast on 11 sts.
Slip 1, k1, p2, k2, p2, k2, p1 and purl to end.
Next row RS facing, knit 30 sts. (k2, p2) repeat once, k2, p1.
Continue working offset 2x2 rib at pocket opening until 52 pocket rows have been worked. Turn and cast off 11 sts, break off yarn leaving a length of about 12 in (30 cm) at the pocket edge and place remaining 30 sts on hold.

Make pocket lining: cast on 30 sts. Work 23 rows in st st. At end of 23rd row (RS until facing) knit on the sts held for front and continue in st st for 30 rows.
Tip: it may be easier to pin or tack the pocket lining in place at this stage.

Cast off 3 sts at pocket edge on next and following 9 alternate rows (30 sts in total)
Tip: slip first of cast off sts through back of loop each time to get a smooth edge.
WS facing, work 25, 29, 33 sts. Continue to work across the 30 sts on hold with main yarn joining the two sections together. Tack pocket and edge in place with contrast thread (to unpick and press before final sewing).

Continue until front measures same as back to armhole (58 cm (23 in) or required length). Work armhole shaping as for Back. Then cast off 1 more st at armhole edge (39, 43, 47 sts remaining). Continue until right front measures 67 cm (26 in).

Shape neck: cast off at neck edge 5, 4, 3, 2, 1 sts on alternate rows (24, 28, 32 sts remaining, which is (2, 1, 1) sts more than the back shoulder shaping). Continue until front measures same as back to shoulder. Cast off over 3 alternate rows to match back shaping.

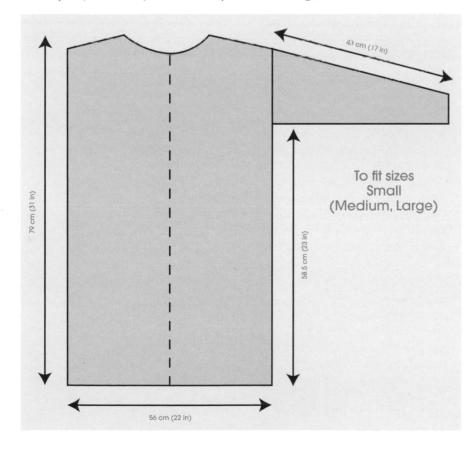

79 cm (31 in)

56 cm (22 in)

43 cm (17 in)

58.5 cm (23 in)

To fit sizes
Small
(Medium, Large)

LEFT FRONT
(make one)

Work as right front to pocket opening.
RS facing, knit 25 29, 33 sts. Cast on 11 into next st for pocket edge
NOTE: to get an exact match at the pocket edge this side is worked as follows, starting with the cast on sts.
Row 1: s1, p1, k2, p2, k2, p2, k1, k to end.
Row 2: p 30 sts, k2, p2, k2, p2, k2, p1
Continue working offset 2x2 rib at pocket opening until 52 pocket rows have been worked. Place these sts on a spare needle or holder.

Make pocket lining. Cast on 30 sts. **Starting with a purl row,** work 24 rows.
Next row: WS facing, purl across pocket lining and continue across 25, 29, 33 held sts.
Continue to match right front reversing all shapings.

SLEEVES
(make two)

Join shoulder seam. With 4 mm (size 6) needles and right side facing, pick up and knit 123 sts from armhole edge. Change to 4.5 mm (size 7) needles and work in stocking stitch.
Row 1 (with right side facing)**:** K2tog, k1, (k2tog, k2) 5 times, k28 (k2tog, k2) 5 times, k28, (k2tog, k2) 6 times. 106 sts.
Row 2 and all alternate rows**:** purl if using two needles, or knit if using a circular needle.
Row 3: (k2, k2tog) 3 times. k37, (k2tog) 3 times, k39 (k2tog,k2) 3 times. 97 sts.
Row 5: Knit
Row 7: K2, (k2tog,k1) 3 times. K to last 10 sts,

(k2tog, k1) 3 times, k1. 91 sts.
Row 9: Knit.
Row 11: K2, (k2tog) 3 times, k to the last 8 sts, (k2tog) 3 times, k2. 85 sts.
Row 13: Knit.
Row 15: K2, k2tog, k to last 4 sts, k2tog, k2. 83 sts.
Continue to decrease 1 st at each end of every following 6th row as set until 63 sts are left on needle.
Work 4 more rows (or adjust length here).
If making the tight cuff change to 4 mm (size 6) needles, and decrease 3 sts evenly on first row working in k2, p2rib for 5 in (13 cm). Cast off in rib.
If working the looser cuff in off-set rib, change to 4 mm (size 6) needles and work in rib for 26 cm (10 in), if using one colour, or 13 cm (5 in) in main colour and 13 cm (5 in) in contrast colour. Cast off in rib.

NOTE: work the offset rib as follows:
Row 1: SL1, *k2, p2*, repeat from * to * to last 4 sts, k2, p1, k1
All subsequent rows: as row 1
Please remember when picking up stitches that this design works for multiples of 4 sts plus 1 only.

COLLAR (make one)

Using 4 mm (size 6) needles and with RS facing pick up 41 (43, 45) sts between centre front and shoulder, 8 (9, 10) sts at side of back neck, 24 sts from holder (pick up 2 of these as one st to make the offset rib work with an uneven number of sts), 8 (9, 10) to shoulder and 41 (43, 45) to centre front. Work offset rib for 10 cm (4 in). Change to contrast colour if used, work 10 cm (4 in). Cast off firmly in rib.

CENTRE BANDS
(make two)

Pick up 120 sts between bottom of welt and half way up on collar on each of the fronts. Add/reduce number of sts if length of garment has been increased/reduced.
For buttonhole band: *K2, P2* repeat to end. Work 4 rows. Work 7 buttonholes to fit your chosen buttons, evenly spaced along next row. Continue until 9 rows have been worked. Cast off in rib.
For button band: row 1 *P2, K2* repeat to end. Check bands to make sure that rib pattern is knitted evenly and will meet correctly with buttonhole side. Work to 9 rows. Cast off in rib.

MAKING UP

Turn down collar onto wrong side, pin in place matching pattern. Sew down firmly. Neaten ends. With contrast wool, tack the buttonhole band into place over the button band to match exactly and sew on buttons at buttonholes (do this after washing and pressing the garment to be more certain of a perfect match). Sew up side seams (leaving slits at the bottom welt if desired). If wide cuffs have been made, turn under off-set rib cuff and stitch in place. Sew seams.

Autumn leaves beret

By Rita Taylor

This attractive beret is made with dyed Gotland Double Knitting yarn and has a lacy, leaf-shaped motif, with twelve leaves falling from the crown to the brim.

It is made in one size and is reasonably stretchy, but if you need to alter it slightly, use one size larger or smaller knitting needles. If you need to alter it by more than this, increase or decrease in multiples of eight stitches to accommodate the design.

The worsted-weight DK yarn is used doubled throughout. Use one colour, or two closely toned shades, or the lace pattern will be lost. This is a great starting point for first-time lace knitters.

DESIGNER PROFILE

Rita Taylor has been a keen knitter since childhood and is interested in traditonal Scottish patterns. She recreates ganseys for the British Knitting & Crochet Guild.

YARN REQUIREMENTS

Gotland worsted-weight DK yarn
• Total amount of wool by weight and approximate length:
100 g/220 m (238 yds)
• Use yarn doubled throughout

Method

Using 3.75 mm (size 5) needles, cast on 101 sts.
Work in p3 k1 rib, beginning first row with p2, until work measures 5 cm (2 in) from cast on edge. Change to 5 mm (size 8) needles and continue for a further 5 cm (2 in).

Start pattern:
Row 1: P2 (yf, k1, yrn, p2) to end.
Row 2: K2 (p3, k2) to end.
Row 3: P2 (k1, yf, k1, yf, p3tog) to last 2 sts, p2.
Row 4: K4 (p5, k1) to last 4, k4.
Row 5: P4 (k2, yf, k1, yf, k2, p5) to last 4, p4.
Row 6: K4 (p7, k5) to end.
Row 7: P4 (k3, yf, k1, yf, k3, p5) to end.
Row 8: K4 (p9, k5) to end.
Row 9: P4 (k9, p5) to end.
Row 10: as row 8.
Row 11: as row 9.
Row 12: as row 8.
Row 13: P4 (ssk, k5, k2tog, p5) to end.
Row 14: as row 6.
Row 15: P4 (ssk, k3, k2tog, p5) to end.
Row 16: K4 (p5, k5) to last 4, k4.
Row 17: P4 (ssk, k1, k2tog, p5) to end.
Row 18: K4 (p3, k5) to end.
Row 19: P1, p2tog (p1, sl1, k2tog, psso) to last 4, p1, p2tog, p1.
Row 20: K1, ssk (p1, k1) to last 3, k2tog, k1.
Row 21: K1, p1 to last st, k1.
Row 22: P1, k1 to last st, p1.
Row 23: K1, p3tog, to last st, k1.
Row 24: P1, k1 to last st, p1.
Row 25: K1 (p1, sl1 k2tog, psso) to end.
Break off wool leaving a tail of about 40 cm (16 in). Thread wool through remaining sts, draw up and fasten off. Use remaining wool to sew back seam.

MEASUREMENTS
One size to fit an average adult head (53 cm (21 in) approx)

NEEDLES & NOTIONS
One pair 3.75 mm (size 5) and 5 mm (size 8) needles

TENSION
Approx 20 sts x 24 rows = 10 cm (4 in) using doubled yarn over stocking stitch on 5 mm (size 8) needles
Adjust needle size to give required tension.

ABBREVIATIONS (see also page 140)
ssk: (slip, slip, knit) slip 2 stitches knitwise from the left to the right needle, then insert the tip of the left needle into the fronts of the slipped stitches and knit them together from this position.
yf: wrap the yarn over the needle, to create an extra stitch on the return row and a small lace hole (knit stitches).
yrn: bring yarn forward, take over the needle and then back to the front of the work again, to create an extra stitch on the return row and a small lace hole (purl stitches).

Hebridean fleece

The hardy Hebridean sheep is gaining a special place in British conservation grazing, as it manages with very little human intervention, including producing one or two lambs each year. It is probably not a true native: the black genes appear to have come from the Middle East and managed to reach northern Europe over the centuries as merchants travelled and traded livestock.

The fleece of the Hebridean sheep is completely black, but gradually gains grey hairs with age, so that it is possible to make grey yarns and weave them into striped rug designs. It may also be bleached brown by the sun. The type of fleece varies: some are soft and fine, others are more dense.

Originally, most small, native Scottish sheep were northern short-tailed breeds with brown faces. They were descended from Iron Age breeds, and known as Dunface sheep. Being small, they became minorities on the highlands and were eventually found only on the islands. The modern sheep dates from the 9th century.

Small parkland sheep such as the Hebridean have not proved to be commercially viable for meat or wool and used to rely on hobby farmers for their existence. Recently, ewes have been cross-bred for better meat production. The meat is recognised as lean, healthy and tasty. If bred with rams with white genes, the lambs are white, which results in more profitable wool production. Ewes grow to 35–40 kg (77–88 lbs) and rams to 50–55 kg (110–121 lbs).

When intensive farming developed after 1945 Hebridean numbers fell. By 1973, it was designated 'rare' by the Rare Breeds Survival Trust. However, its success at conservation grazing means it no longer requires preservation, and is now listed as a Native Breed. No flocks are recorded in the US.

BREED AT A GLANCE

Sheep type: Primitive, northern short-tailed.
Appearance: Small, with black fleece and imposing horns (a few have four but some ewes have none).
Rare breeds status: Native breed not on the UK at-risk register.
Further information: UK breed society: www.hebrideansheep.org.uk.
History: Descended from a flock of wild native sheep taken from the island of Uist in the 1880s and selected and bred as black for parkland grazing in Cumbria.

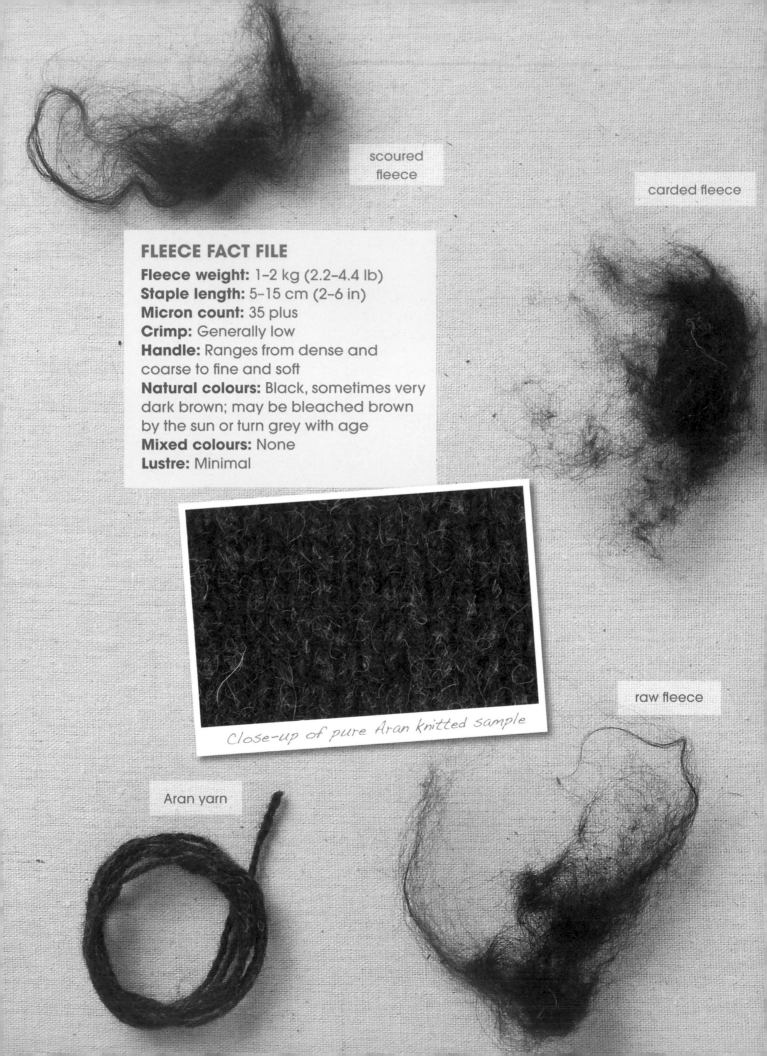

scoured
fleece

carded fleece

FLEECE FACT FILE
Fleece weight: 1–2 kg (2.2–4.4 lb)
Staple length: 5–15 cm (2–6 in)
Micron count: 35 plus
Crimp: Generally low
Handle: Ranges from dense and
coarse to fine and soft
Natural colours: Black, sometimes very
dark brown; may be bleached brown
by the sun or turn grey with age
Mixed colours: None
Lustre: Minimal

Close-up of pure Aran knitted sample

raw fleece

Aran yarn

Hebridean yarn

Hebridean wool is often a dull black in colour, without much lustre. Once it begins to grey with age, or to be bleached by the sun, it can be quite a flat off-black bitter chocolate colour, with plenty of kempy fibres.

Wool from a Hebridean lamb or shearling is softer and slightly lustrous when compared with that of an adult sheep. If this is not available, an older fleece can be improved by blending it with mohair to produce a lovely soft and shiny charcoal colour, or with Manx Loagthan to provide a rich chocolate brown with great depth. I often use Hebridean wool to add a little colour and texture to the smoother and blander Corriedale or Falkland wools.

However, the fleeces can be matted or contain vegetation, which can be a challenge to spinners, although it will not impede knitters who buy their yarn ready spun!

It is not all bad news though! As it is relatively coarse and straight, the wool has a generally low crimp, but the fleece is dense, strong and springy, making yarns which are hard-wearing, crisp and firm. For example, Hebridean fibres produce a more distinct texture in a fabric made from dark yarn than Black Welsh Mountain. They also make strong weaving yarns and are an excellent way to add natural colour and contrast in rugs and blankets.

Hebridean wool is good too for strong outerwear, bags, cushions and socks. The following patterns are for a handbag and a black-and-white cushion based on traditional Scottish Sanquahar designs. However, the yarn will cheerfully work as a crisper and harder wearing alternative to the patterns for Black Welsh Mountain, Castlemilk Moorit, Jacob, Manx Loagthan and North Ronaldsay, as well as Ryeland or Zwartbles yarns.

YARN USER'S GUIDE
Good for ...
- Weaving
- Durable knitted items such as outerwear, and bags and socks
- Blankets and rugs
- Felting

Not so good for ...
- Dyeing
- Lightweight items
- Wearing next to the skin

Dark and lustrous, yarn from from the fleece of the Hebridean sheep makes a durable fabric ideal for hard-wearing outer garments, rugs and bags.

Hebridean handbag

By Sue Blacker

This stylish and chunky bag is designed either to sit neatly under the arm, resting just above the hip, or as a satchel to carry A4-sized documents and files. There is also an option to knit it with a curved base for a modern, slouchy style.

You start by knitting the strap – which also acts as the base and sides of the bag – and then add panels for the front and back (which extends over the front to act as the flap). The strap is decorated with a simple cable stitch, which is a perfect introduction to cable knitting for the beginner, and will please more experienced knitters by being easy to knit as the work grows. Adjust the length of the strap to suit your style – measure an existing bag and work accordingly.

The bag is closed using a button and loop fastening. This can be replaced with a large press stud covered with a tassel. Or make a bag without a flap and close with a button and loop across the top opening.

Two strands of Aran yarn are used for a chunky finish, so you can use a single colour or mix two shades for a tweedy effect. You could also try making the strap in a single colour and the body of the bag in mixed colours

YARN REQUIREMENTS

Hebridean Aran wool
• Total amount of wool by weight and approximate length:
Handbag 350 g/490 m (532 yds)
Shoulder or slouch bag 650 g/910 m (988 yds)

or a contrasting colour. The two strands of chunky wool also make it quick to knit.

Advanced knitters can adapt the pattern, using a provisional cast-on for the strap and then casting off the two ends of the strap together once the bag has

been made up. A further adaptation would be to pick up and work the stitches for the front and back from the strap, joining the panels to the strap as they go. This will result in a very unstructured bag – stitched side seams will create a more rigid bag.

Method

THE STRAP

Using 5 mm (size 8) needles and two strands of wool, cast on 23 sts. Work in cable pattern as follows:

Row 1: S1, k1, p2, k15, p2, k2.
Row 2: S1, p1, k2, p15, k2, p1, k1.
Row 3: S1, k1, p2, k3, C6F, C6F, p2, k2.
Row 4: as row 2.
Row 5: as row 1.
Row 6: as row 2.
Row 7: S1, k1, p2, C6B, C6B, k3, p2, k2.
Row 8: as row 2.

Repeat rows 1-8 until work measures 107 cm (42 in) for handbag or 183 cm (72 in) for shoulder bag. Cast off.

Marking the position of the front and back on the strap

On a flat surface, spread out the strap, right side facing (cable pattern towards you). The seam joining the strap will be at one corner of the base of the bag.

MEASUREMENTS

Handbag: 25 cm (10 in) wide and 15 cm (6 in) deep. Strap measures 46 cm (18 in)
Shoulder and slouch bag: 30 cm (12 in) high and 25 cm (10 in) wide. Strap measures 91.5 cm (36 in)

NEEDLES & NOTIONS

1 pair needles 5 mm (size 8)
Cable needle
Stitch markers (or safety pins)
1 crochet needle 5 mm (size 8)
1 pair double-pointed needles 4 mm (size 6)
Darning needle
1 large button.

TENSION

Approx 13 sts x 17 rows = 10 cm (4 in) over stocking stitch using two strands of wool on 5 mm (size 8) needles
Tension is not particularly important as this design is measured throughout and the pieces can be fitted together as made.

ABBREVIATIONS (see also page 140)

C6F: slip next 3 stitches onto cable needle, hold at front of work, k3 then k sts from cable needle.
C6B: slip next 3 stitches onto cable needle, hold at back of work, k3 then k sts from cable needle.

SKILL LEVEL

HANDBAG

Working from left to right, place a marker at 30 cm (12 in) (marker A), 15 cm (6 in) (marker B), 46 cm (18 in) (marker C). Adjust the measurement between markers B and C so there is 15 cm (6 in) left at the end.
The portion of strap between the end and A marks the base, A to B is one side panel, B to C is the strap, and C to the other end is the second side panel.

Handbag strap dimensions			
start a	b	c	
30cm	15cm	46cm	15cm
12 in	6 in	18 in	6 in
Base	Side	Strap	Side

SHOULDER BAG

Working from left to right, place a marker at 30 cm (12 in) (marker A), 30 cm (12 in) (marker B), 91.5 cm (36 in) (marker C). Adjust the measurement between markers B and C so there is 15 cm (6 in) left at the end.
The portion of strap between the end and A marks the base, A to B is one side panel, B to C is the strap, and C to the other end is the second side panel.

Shoulder bag strap dimensions			
start a	b	c	
30cm	30cm	91.5cm	30cm
12 in	12 in	36 in	12 in
Base	Side	Strap	Side

SLOUCH BAG

The base and sides are stitched to the rounded edge of the bag. Simply divide the strap in half so that the join is in the middle of the base when sewing up.

HAND- AND SHOULDER BAG FRONT (knit 1)

With cable pattern facing upwards, and using crochet hook and two strands of wool, pick up 42 sts from start to A. Insert the hook through the holes of the knit stitches to give a neat finish. Transfer the stitches onto a knitting needle.
Work in stocking stitch until knitting measures 15 cm (6 in) for handbag or 30 cm (12 in) for shoulder bag, ending with a purl row. Cast off.

HAND- AND SHOULDER BAG BACK AND FLAP (knit 1)

With cable pattern facing upwards, and using crochet hook and two strands of wool, pick up 42 sts from other side of the strap from start to A, in the same way as for the front. Work in stocking stitch until knitting measures 15 cm (6 in) for handbag or 30 cm (12 in) for shoulder bag. Place a marker at the end of this row. This forms the back and the extent to which you will need to sew the back to the sides of the bag. Continue knitting for a further 15 cm (6 in) ending with a purl row.

Shaping the flap

Next row: K3, s1, k1, psso. Knit to last 5 sts, s1, k1, psso, k3.
Next row: purl.
Repeat these two rows 6 times (30 sts remain). Cast off. The flap will roll up of its own accord; sew this back into place at either end.

SLOUCH BAG FRONT (make 1)

With 2 strands of yarn, cast on 8sts.
Row 1: purl
Row 2 (RS): knit to last stitch, cast on 8 sts
Row 3: purl to last stitch, cast on 8 sts
Row 4: knit
Row 5: purl
Row 6: as row 2
Row 7: as row 3
Row 8: knit
Row 9: purl
Row 10: (RS) knit to last stitch, cast on 4 sts
Row 11: purl to last stitch, cast on 4 sts
Repeat non increase and increase rows with 4 sts increase for next 4 rows, then with 3 sts increase for next 8 rows and 2 st increase for next 8 rows to make a total of 76 sts.

Now continue in stocking stitch until work measures 25 cm (10 in) from cast on edge. Cast off.

SLOUCH BAG BACK (make 1)

Work as for front, but instead of casting off when work measures 25 cm (10 in)), place a marker at the end of this row. This forms the back and the extent to which you will need to sew the back to the sides of the bag. Continue work for a further 15 cm (6 in) ending with a purl row. Shape flap as for shoulder bag.

FINISHING OFF

Hand- and shoulder bag
With right sides facing, sew back and front to sides, using markers as a guide. Sew on a large button in the centre of the front approx 7 cm (2.5 in) from the base.

Slouch bag
Mark centre of base on front and back. Join strap ends, then pin to front, matching the centre of the base to the join in the strap. Repeat for the back. You can hide the seams inside the bag, or keep them on the outside as a feature, in which case use back stitch.

Crochet or knit an I-cord, or plait some wool to make a cord approx 5 cm (2 in) long with a tail of 10 cm (4 in) on each side and sew on to the base of the flap to provide a fastening for the button. Sew the loop together at the top

KNITTER PROFILE

Sarah Shourie began knitting at the age of five and knitted several designs for this book. She finds single-breed yarns a joy to use as they work well on the needles.

so that it will fasten around the button tightly.
Wash bag. Block to dry, or dry flat and steam press to correct shape when dry.
To stiffen the base more, cut two lengths of drinking straw or wood skewer and oversew into each corner across the width of the base.

Sanquhar cushion

By Tina Barrett

Sanquhar knitting designs developed in the town of that name in Dumfries and Galloway, Scotland. The traditional two-colour designs date from the 1700s and were named after people, events and everyday things including The Duke, Rose, Trellis, Drum, Coronet, Glendyne, Midge and Flea, Shepherd's Plaid and Prince of Wales, and Fleur de Lys. They were knitted in the round to create items such as gloves and stockings and sold to bring vital income to many families.

This cushion takes two traditional geometric Sanquhar stitch patterns and reinterprets them for flat knitting to make an attractive cushion in Hebridean and white wool (we have used white Jacob yarn).

The front is worked as a single piece and the back as two pieces, which meet in the middle, and may be finished with a zip or buttons or hooks and loops.

YARN REQUIREMENTS

• Total amount of wool by weight and approximate length

Yarn A: Pure Hebridean Wool DK 200 g/440 m (476 yds)
Yarn B: Pure Pale Jacob Wool DK 100 g/220 m (238 yds)

Method

FRONT (make one)

Using 4 mm (size 6) needles and Hebridean yarn (A), cast on 95 sts.

Work 2 rows in stocking stitch, then joining in Jacob yarn (B) work as follows:

Row 1: K10, work 24 sts of Row 1 of the Duke chart (right hand border), work 27 sts of Row 1 of the Midge and Fly chart, work 24 sts of Row 1 of the Duke chart (left hand border), k10.
Row 2: p10, work 24 sts of Row 2 of the Duke chart (left hand border), work 27 sts of Row 2 of the Midge and Fly chart, work

24 sts of Row 2 of the Duke chart (right hand border), p10.
These 2 rows set the pattern for the cushion front.

Continue to work the chart repeats until you have completed the Duke borders 4 times. Then, continue as set until you have completed 12 further rows of the Duke border.

Work 2 rows in stocking stitch using Hebridean (A).
Bind/cast off.

BACK (make two)

Using Hebridean (A) and 4 mm (size 6) needles, cast on 97 sts.
Work as follows using the 2 colours stated in brackets:
Row 1: P2(A), *k3(B), p2(A)* repeat from * to * to end of row.
Row 2: K2(A), *p3(B), k2(A)* repeat from * to * to end of row.
Row 3: P2(A), * k1(B),k1(A),k1(B), p2(A)* repeat from * to * to end of row.
Row 4: As Row 2.
Repeat Rows 1-4 once more, then work Rows 1 and 2 once.

Change to Hebridean (A) and work in stocking stitch for a further 22 cm (8.5 in) ending with a purl row.
Bind/cast off.

FINISHING

Darn in loose yarn ends.
Pin and block pieces into shape.

With right sides facing, place the two back flaps over the front piece, overlapping the ribbed bands and lining up all edges. Pin and then sew along all sides. Turn right side out, insert cushion pad through back flap. Or, sew along three sides. Attach zip, hooks or buttons and loops to fourth side. Turn right side out and insert cushion pad then close fastening.

MEASUREMENTS
Finished cushion size:
41 x 41 cm (16 x 16 in) square

NEEDLES & NOTIONS
A pair of 4 mm (size 6) needles
41 cm (16 in) cushion pad
Zip, buttons or hooks (optional)

TENSION
25 sts x 26 rows = 10 cm (4 in) using 4 mm (size 6) needles over Duke and Midge and Fly stitch pattern.
22 sts x 30 rows = 10 cm (4 in) using 4 mm (size 6) needles over stocking stitch.

SKILL LEVEL

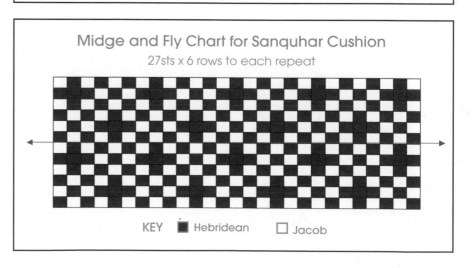

Sanquhar Cushion Charts for Duke Design Side Borders
Midge and Fly Chart will sit between the borders at point of red arrow.
Duke Design Charts 24 sts x 25 rows each

Left side border   Right side border

KEY ■ Hebridean □ Jacob

Midge and Fly Chart for Sanquhar Cushion
27sts x 6 rows to each repeat

KEY ■ Hebridean □ Jacob

Herdwick fleece

Perhaps because the eyes are set more to the front than on many sheep, or perhaps because the head is relatively rounded, the Herdwick has one of the most distinctive and attractive sheep faces. They are considered the hardiest of British breeds and are said to resort to eating their own fleeces if necessary when there is too much snow or too little grass.

Herdwick sheep have a heavy, dense fleece with a fine undercoat, coarser fibres and kemp and sometimes a stronger ruffle or mane at the neck and shoulders. This coat is adapted for the harsh weather of their traditional home, the high, exposed and rain-swept Cumbrian fells of the Lake District. Farmers find the fleece dries out faster than that of other breeds after rain.

They are free to roam over long distances to find enough to eat and have a unique inherited knowledge of the fells, known as 'heaf'. This tells them which areas of the hills – much like an upland desert to a stranger – their flock has traditionally grazed and enables them to navigate their way home. No: sheep are not stupid!

Like many mountain sheep, the Herdwick spends time tupping and lambing in the valleys. The lambs and ewes return to the hills after lambing, and the ewes spend the winter on the hills. Ram lambs are fattened in the valley; ewe lambs are kept there to gain strength.

A famous Herdwick farmer was the children's author and illustrator Beatrix Potter, who farmed around Hawkshead. At her death in 1943, she left all her fifteen farms of 16 square kilometres (4,000 acres) of land to the National Trust to be grazed by Herdwick sheep.

Solidly built with sturdy legs, the Herdwick is not a large sheep and weighs in at 35–45 kg (77–99 lbs) for ewes and 65–75 kg (143–165 lbs) for rams.

BREED AT A GLANCE

Sheep type: Native breed.
Appearance: The rams generally have curling horns but the ewes have none. White heads and legs; born dark brown or black, gradually fading through grey to white as they get older.
Rare breeds status: Vulnerable.
Further information:
UK breed society: www.herdwick-sheep.com.
History: Recorded from the 12th century. They are thought variously to originate from Viking imports or the Spanish Armada. Unlike the other sheep inhabiting the high western pastures of the UK, they are not part of the northern short-tail family.

Aran yarn overdyed purple

scoured fleece

Close-up of knitted Aran sample

raw fleece

Aran yarn overdyed olive

carded fleece

Aran yarn overdyed plum

Herdwick yarn

Herdwick fleece is coarse and dense, and although there is some soft undercoat, most of it is quite harsh, thick, and stiff. Nevertheless, the colour is one of the most attractive, being varied in whites, greys, and browns, so yarns and felt have a wonderful depth of natural tweedy colours.

The thick fleeces, with their relatively short staple length, can only be used for woollen spinning and are best used for thicker, Aran or chunky yarns. The lovely natural colours are ideal for rugs and carpets, and also for hard-wearing woven travel rugs. The fleece contains kempy fibres which do not take dye, but give the dyed yarns a lovely heathery result.

Writing with the experience of having knitted and worn a Herdwick pullover, I can certainly say it is possible, but most people will find the wool too scratchy. So we have chosen accessories to show off the colour and texture of the yarn in the home, with tea and coffee cosies. However, Herdwick yarn will also work on bags, cushions, and hard-wearing body-warmers and waistcoats, so the patterns for the Hebridean bag, Jacob socks and North Ronaldsay would also work. If blended with mohair, the wool will take dye even better and becomes softer.

YARN USER'S GUIDE

Good for ...
- Carpets
- Felting
- Outerwear
- Home accessories
- Woven rugs

Not so good for ...
- Wearing next to the skin
- Dyeing for solid colours

Dyed Herdwick yarn has an appealing heathery appearance thanks to the kemp in the fleece.

Herdwick tea, cafetière, and egg cosies

By Sue Blacker

This very easy design is made to measure for your cafetière or teapot. Each item can be finished with a pom-pom or tassels. The originals were designed using a combination of dyed and naturally coloured yarn, but you can choose just Herdwick Hog (brown) and older Herdwick (grey and/or white) if you prefer, and use one, two or three colours, as available.

The design has only one pattern row, and instructions are given to make stripes, using three colours in turn, but you can use a single colour or stripes of as many colours as you like! Striped items normally need joins between the colours, but we have used narrow stripes so that you can just carry the spare colour up the side of the work to save breaking off and re-joining all the time.

To carry the yarn up the side of the work neatly, pass the yarn not being used between the first slipped stitch of the row from front to back at the beginning of each odd numbered row (i.e. where the strands are!).

You will need to take care not to get in a tangle, but it is not difficult! It is easier to take yarn from the centre of a ball, not the outside.

To get started, you must measure the cafetière or teapot for which you are making the cosy and use this to calculate the stitches and rows required. You can

YARN REQUIREMENTS

Herdwick Aran yarn
• Total amount of wool by weight and approximate length for tea and cafetière cosies: 3 x 50g/70 m (76 yds) Use spare yarn for the egg cosies.
The yarn is used double throughout.

also use the dimensions of an existing cosy. Don't worry if your measurements are not exact – a little bit too big is

Method

TEA COSY
Worked in two pieces, and then seamed up each side, leaving space for the handle and spout. The width of each side is half the circumference of the pot. Add 3 cm (1.5 in) for easing to both sides. For example, if the pot is 40 cm (15.5 in) around, your knitting will be 23 cm (9 in) wide (half of 40 cm (15.5 in) plus 3 cm (1.5 in)).

CAFETIÈRE COSY
Worked in one piece, and covers the whole cafetière (it is removed for pouring). The width of your knitting will be the circumference of the cafetière including the handle. Add 3 cm (1.5 in) for easing to both sides. For example, if the pot is 40 cm (15.5 in) around, your knitting will be 46 cm (17 in) wide 40 cm plus 6 cm (15.75 in plus 1.5 in).

TEA AND CAFETIÈRE COSIES
Measure the overall height of the teapot or cafetière, from the base to the centre of the lid. This will be the length to knit. If you want, make it 10 cm (4 in) longer to turn over the rim.

PATTERN
Tweedy stripes: start in your first two colours (A and B, whichever you prefer), knit 2 rows, then drop A and add in the next colour, C, knit 2 rows, then drop the B, to add in the A again and knit 2 rows, and so you have 6 rows, with the first 2 in A and B, the second 2 in B and C and the third 2 in C and A, then go back to A and B and repeat the process. Continue, changing colour every two rows. The ends and balls of wool will always be at one side of the work.
Plain stripes: use 2 strands of A, followed by 2 strands of B, then 2 strands of C and work 2 rows in each colour. (Or use two colours if prefered.)

SIDES (knit 1 or 2)
Using 6 mm (size 10) needles and two strands of yarn, cast on 10 sts loosely for every 5 cm (2 in) of your side measurement (e.g. if the circumference is 20 cm (8 in), cast on 40 sts; if 15 cm (6 in), then it is 30 sts; if 25 cm (10 in), it is 50 sts, etc.). *This pattern only works with multiples of 4 sts plus 1*, so add on extra sts to make this work (e.g. for 15 cm (6 in)), which would need 30 sts, make it 33, and for 40 and 50 stitches, make it 41 and 53, etc.)
Row 1: SL1, *k2, p2*, repeat from * to * to last 4 sts, k2, p1, k1. All following rows, as Row 1 using narrow striped pattern as described above.
Continue until work measures the correct length. Bind off.

EGG COSY
These are worked with a single strand of yarn. Make in one colour and add pom-poms in a contrasting colour. Or make stripes from spare yarn. Make a different colour – or pattern – for each family member!

SIDES (knit 1)
Using 6 mm (size 10) needles and your chosen colour, cast on 29 sts loosely.
Row 1: SL1, *k2, p2*, repeat from * to * to last 4 sts, k2, p1, k1.
All following rows, as Row 1 Continue with pattern and stripes until work measures 10 am (4 in) long. Bind off.

MAKING UP
Break off yarn, leaving a long thread, and use a darning needle to thread through your stitches and pull up tightly to gather at the top and overstitch to secure. Using the same thread, sew down the side seam – leaving spaces for the teapot spout and handle – and sewing in any loose ends. Fasten securely. Sew a pom-pom or tassel securely over the centre of the gathered top. (See page 141.)

Jacob fleece

There is only one truly and distinctly spotted sheep: the black-and-white Jacob. They have a characteristic white blaze on the face and a tendency to develop more dark patches at the front than at the back. Some Jacob sheep have a few large dark patches, while a very few are almost like Dalmatian dogs with many small spots.

Little is known about the origins of the Jacob sheep beyond the fact that they came to the UK from the Middle East, possibly via Spain. Spotted sheep can been seen in Egyptian wall paintings dated to 1800 BC.

British breeding has tended to select for larger sheep, to make them more commercial, but the US breeders have focused more on the decorative characteristics, possibly closer to the breed's primitive roots, so the fleeces, sheep and sizes vary. The fact that much less sheep meat is eaten in the US may be a factor in this.

Despite their decorative appearance, Jacob sheep are hardy and a viable commercial breed. A decent size, ewes weigh 60–65 kg (132–143 lbs) and rams 80–100 kg (176–220 lbs).

While it is a minority breed, the sheep are not rare in the UK. However, having been a parkland sheep it was considered to be a hobby animal. When the Rare Breeds Survival Trust was established in 1974, it classified the Jacob as a Minority Breed as there were only 2,000 registered breeding ewes. Today, the Jacob is a success story with more than 5,000 registered ewes. In 1989 there were 400 animals registered in the US By 2006, more than 10,000 Jacob sheep were known, but it is listed as a rare breed by the American Livestock Breeds Conservancy.

BREED AT A GLANCE

Sheep type: Primitive.

Appearance: 2–6 horns, piebald white/black fleece (UK standard is for two-thirds white and one-third black).

Rare breeds status: Threatened in the US. No longer considered at risk in the UK.

Further information: UK breed society: www.jacobsheep.org.uk.
US breed society: www.jsba.org.

History: Claimed to have originated in Mesopotamia in Biblical times, taking its name from Jacob in the Old Testament, who became rich from rearing a flock of spotted sheep. Like other coloured sheep, used as parkland sheep and from the mid-18th century were imported to the UK and the US for this purpose.

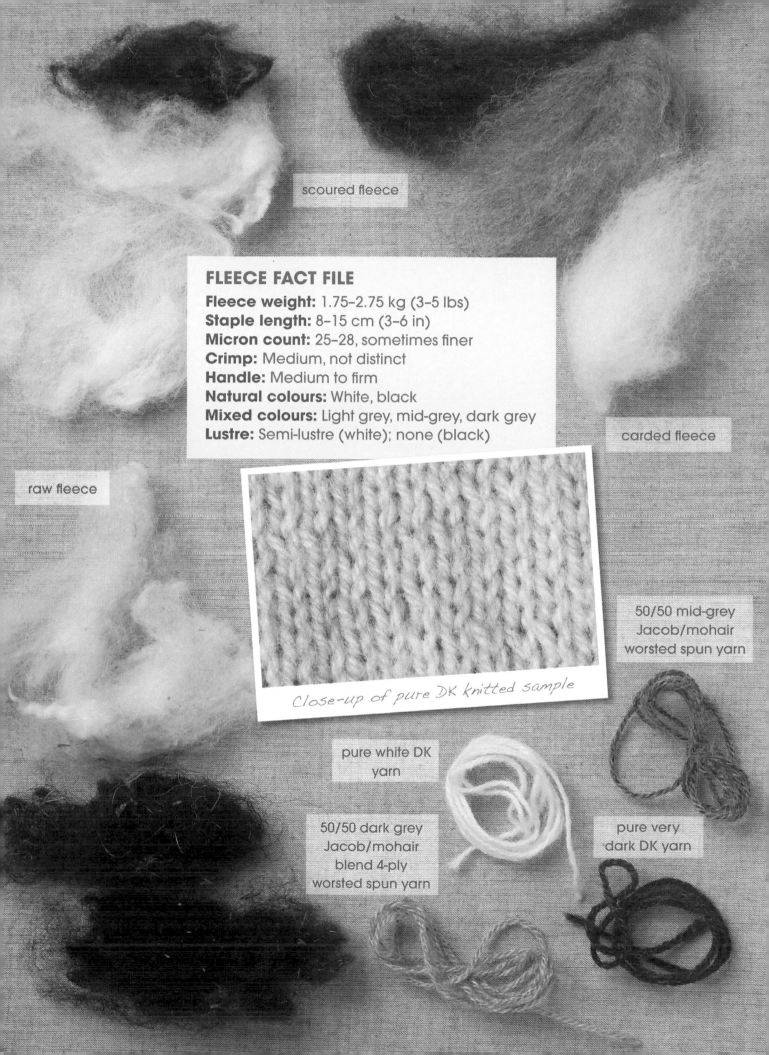

scoured fleece

FLEECE FACT FILE
Fleece weight: 1.75–2.75 kg (3–5 lbs)
Staple length: 8–15 cm (3–6 in)
Micron count: 25–28, sometimes finer
Crimp: Medium, not distinct
Handle: Medium to firm
Natural colours: White, black
Mixed colours: Light grey, mid-grey, dark grey
Lustre: Semi-lustre (white); none (black)

carded fleece

raw fleece

Close-up of pure DK knitted sample

50/50 mid-grey
Jacob/mohair
worsted spun yarn

pure white DK
yarn

50/50 dark grey
Jacob/mohair
blend 4-ply
worsted spun yarn

pure very
dark DK yarn

Jacob yarn

Jacob fleece is of medium thickness, length and softness, and it is incredibly versatile as a result. The only things it is not really suitable for are lace and baby clothes; it is also not as easy to felt as some other fibres.

Although most Jacob wool is 'black and white', the dark colour can be anything from mauve-brown or blue-brown to off-black, and the white wool is a creamy colour. Separating the colours of wool into dark, light and 'in-between' gives three shades: cream, very dark brown and brown-grey. These three can be re-mixed to create at least two further intermediate shades.

There may be significant differences of texture, thickness and even staple length between the white and dark fleece on individual Jacob sheep, although this is considered a defect in fleece judging. For example, the dark wool tends to be coarser, possibly with more kemp and shorter than the pale wool, which also sometimes has quite noticeable lustre. The lock formation may also be different, with the dark wool woollier and with an indistinct crimp, and the pale wavier and with straighter locks.

This range of wool from a single sheep is only matched by the varied colours achieved (but mainly individually) by Shetland sheep. In addition, all paler versions and blends of the colour-sorted Jacob shades will dye happily.

The fleeces are excellent for hand-spinning, and work in both woollen- and worsted-spun yarns, and from 4-ply to chunky weights. However, the Jacob's fibres are too thick and bulky to make a lace-weight yarn.

The wool can be softened by blending with mohair, which not only makes it more hard-wearing but also enhances the lustre and the dyeing results. We have also found that Jacob blends well with alpaca, which makes soft weaving yarns for scarves. Natural Jacob, as well as blends with mohair, make wonderful blankets, throws and shawls.

Jacob is versatile and, apart from the Cotswold and some Gotland or fine Shetland patterns, may be used as an alternative for every pattern in this book! We have chosen a chunky jacket, knitted in two differently coloured strands of double knitting yarn to show off the natural colours, and a pair of socks made in a 50/50 blend of Jacob with mohair for extra wear.

If the many natural shades of Jacob yarn are not enough, it dyes well. Here it is used to knit the cardigan on page 126.

YARN USER'S GUIDE

Good for ...
- Blending, weaving, dyeing
- Hand-spinning
- A wide range of weights of yarn
- Versatile knitting yarn
- Textured and cabled designs (if worsted-spun or Guernsey)

Not so good for ...
- Dyeing darker wool
- Lace-weight yarn
- Baby clothes
- Felting

Jacob cable jacket

By Myra Mortlock

This cosy jacket is quick to knit and makes a perfect introduction to knitting cables. It is worked using two strands of worsted-weight or DK yarn. This means you can choose two different shades to create a tweed effect (as shown in the photographs), or use just one colour. The jacket is also quick to knit.

The body and sleeves have a chunky texture thanks to the garter and moss stitch panels, which frame a central double cable on the back, and cabled edges on the front. The jacket is designed to be closed with a large button – or you can use a brooch or shawl pin.

You can work the collar in moss stitch, which will lie flat, or reverse stocking stitch, which results in an attractive curled edge. Similarly, the centre-front bands can be worked in moss stitch, rather than the garter stitch shown. This will result in flat, rather than curled, edges.

The drape of the jacket can be altered by knitting loosely or more tightly – knit a trial swatch and change needle size to create the effect you want (see notes on Tension).

It is a large garment, and so it becomes quite heavy as is it knitted, but think how warm it will keep you!

YARN REQUIREMENTS

Jacob worsted-weight/DK
• Total amount of wool by weight and approximate length:
Small 900 g/1,980 m (2,165 yds)
Medium 1,000 g/2,200 m (2,405 yds)
Large 1,100 g/2,420 m (2645 yds)
• Yarn used doubled throughout. Use a single colour throughout, or equal amounts of two different colours for a tweedy effect.

Method

NOTE: working with two strands of yarn is easy, but occasionally you will only pick up one, so check each row. You will usually find the mistake on the next row. Use a crochet hook to pick up and link in the extra strand.

BACK (make 1)

With 7 mm (size 10½) needles and two strands of yarn, cast on 69 (75, 81) sts.
First row:
Size S: *k3, p1, k1, p1*, repeat * to * 3 times; set sts for centre cable panel p2, k6, p2, k1, p2, k6, p2; *p1, k1, p1, k3*, repeat * to * 3 times.
Size M: k3, *p1, k1, p1, k3*, repeat * to * 3 times; set sts for centre cable panel p2, k6, p2, k1, p2, k6, p2; *k3, p1, k1, p1*, repeat * to * 3 times, k3.
Size L: *k3, p1, k1, p1*, repeat * to * 4 times; set sts for centre cable panel p2, k6, p2, k1, p2, k6, p2; *p1, k1, p1, k3* repeat * to * 4 times.
Repeat this row, working cable panel on the centre panel sts. Continue until back measures 22 (23, 24) in (56 (58, 61) cm).

Underarm shaping (RS facing and maintaining pattern):
Rows 1 and 2: bind/cast off 3 (4, 5) sts, work to end.
Rows 3 and 4: bind/cast off 2 (3, 4) sts, work to end.
Rows 5 to 10: bind off 1 st, work to end. 53 (55, 57) sts remain.
Continue working in pattern until back measures 30 (31, 32) in (approx 76 (78, 81) cm).
RS facing, work 18 (19, 20) sts. Bind off centre 17 sts.
Work to end.
Working on one shoulder WS facing, work 1 row without shaping. RS facing, s1, k1, psso, work to end.
Repeat these 2 rows.
Work 1 row without shaping.

FINISHED SIZES
Garment bust measurement:
118 (126, 142) cm (46 (50, 56) in)
Length from back of the neck to the hem:
79 (81.5, 84) cm (31 (32, 33) in)
Instructions are given for the smallest size first, followed by medium and large in brackets

SKILL LEVEL	🧶🧶

NEEDLES & NOTIONS
1 pair needles 7 mm (size 10½)
Cable needle
2 stitch holders or lengths of waste yarn
1 large button

TENSION
Approx 12 sts x 16 rows = 10 cm (4 in) over stocking stitch on 7 mm (size 10½) needles
Adjust needle size to give required tension.

ABBREVIATIONS (see also page 140)
C6F: slip 3 sts onto the cable needle. Hold at front of work. K3, then k3 from cable needle.
C6B: slip 3 sts onto cable needle. Hold at back of work. K3, then k3 from cable needle.
Cable panel: Row 1: P2, k6, p2, k1, p2, k6, p2. Row 2: K2, p6, k2, p1, k2, p6, p2. Repeat except for Row 5 and every following 12 row when RS facing: P2, C6B, p2, k1, p2, C6F, p2.

Bind off 16 (17, 18) sts. Complete other shoulder, reversing the shaping.

FRONTS (make 2)

Note: the front side seam edges are worked in moss st. The centre front bands are worked in garter st. The shoulder seam lies about 2 cm (1 in) towards the back, and the cable panel is extended to wrap around and graft together at centre back neck. To make a neat edge to the neckline, slip the first st on each row as follows: s1, p4, k6, p2tog, p1 and continue in pattern.

Start with right front, which has an integrated buttonhole band. With 7 mm (size 10½) needles and two strands of yarn, cast on 42 (45, 48) sts.
Row 1: Sizes S and L: k5, p2, k6, p2, *p1, k1, p1, k3* Repeat to last 3 sts p1, k1, p1.
Size M: k5, p2, k6, p2, *k3, p1, k1, p1* Repeat to end.
Work rows 2–4 in pattern as set.
Row 5: RS facing, k5, p2, C6F, p2, work in pattern to end.
Repeat C6F every 12th row.
Continue until work measures 38 cm (15 in).
Work buttonhole as follows:
RS facing, k3, turn and working on these 3 sts, k4 rows. Break yarn, leaving about 10 cm (4 in) tail of yarn.
Rejoin yarn to main knitting, and, continuing to work cable pattern every 12 rows, work 5 rows. WS facing, work across all sts. Work a further 4 rows.

Shape V-neck by decreasing at front edge and between the cable panel and the main pattern as follows:
RS facing, s1, k1, psso, k3, p2, k6, p2 together, p1, continue in

pattern to end. Work all WS rows in pattern and without shaping.
Next RS row: s1, k1, psso, k2, p2, k6, p2tog, p1, work to end of row in pattern.
Following RS row: at this point the garter st buttonhole band changes to reverse st st to create a roll-over edge for the neck line.
Continue decreasing on alternate rows until 34 (35, 36) sts remain.
Work without shaping until piece measures same as the back to underarm shaping.

Shape armhole
WS facing bind off 3 sts. Work in pattern to end.
Work 1 row.
Next WS row bind off 2 sts.
Work 1 row.
Next 3 WS rows: bind off 1 st at start of row. 27 (28, 29) sts remain.

Shape shoulder and back neck.
Continue working in pattern until front measures the same as the back to shoulder shaping, then work a further 3 or 4 rows so that you end at armhole edge. Bind off 15 (16, 17) sts.
Continue on remaining 12 sts in cable and rollover

edge for a further 7.5 cm (3 in). Cut wool, leaving about 38 cm (15 in) and place sts on a length of spare wool or a stitch holder.

The left front is worked in the same way as the right front, reversing pattern and shaping, so that the cable edge and V-neck are in the centre, and omitting the buttonhole. This means that the first row will start with cable and moss stitch panels and end p2, k6, p2, k5.

SLEEVES (make 2)
With 7 mm (size 10½) needles and two strands of yarn, cast on 45 (48, 51) sts.
All sizes: work 5 rows garter st for cuff.
Change to garter and moss st panels as set for the back.
Continue until sleeve measures 23 (20, 18) cm (9 (8, 7) in).
Increase 1 st at both ends of the next row.
Repeat increase row every 4 cm (1.5 in) until there are 55 (60, 63) sts.
Work on these sts until sleeve measures 40.5 (42, 43) cm

(16 (16.5, 17) in). If you would like the cuff to end at the knuckle, rather than the wrist, work a further 2.5 cm (1 in).
Shape to match armhole shaping by decreasing at the start of rows as follows:
Rows 1 and 2: bind off 4 sts.
Rows 3 and 4: bind off 3 sts.
Rows 5 and 6: bind off 2 sts.
Rows 7 and 8 bind off 1 st.
Work 2 rows. Then repeat rows 7 and 8. Repeat * to * twice.
Bind off 3 sts at the beginning of the next 2 rows, then 5 sts at the start of the following 2 rows.
Bind off all remaining sts.

MAKING UP
Join shoulder seams. Attach sleeves to armhole edges. Sew side and sleeve seams.
Adjust length of cable bands if needed so that they meet at centre back neck. Place cable band sts back on needles, both pointing the same way. Using cable needle, join pieces by knitting together a st from each needle and casting off in the usual way. Join cable band to back so that join lies above centre back.

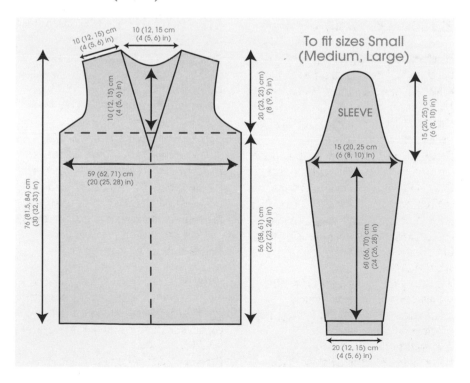

Socks for walking and welly boots

By Sue Blacker

This versatile pattern makes a great introduction to sock knitting. The socks are knitted from the top down and – apart from getting used to knitting on three needles rather than two – the pattern instructions are very simple to follow.

If you have never knitted a sock before, the heel instructions may not make a great deal of sense, but stick with them – if you do as indicated, the heel will turn.

There is no need to use a special sock yarn: any 4-ply yarn can be used for the walking boot socks, and choose an Aran yarn for the rain boot version.

Make them in any solid Jacob colour, or try stripes all over the sock or just on the turnover of the rain boot design. If you're planning to make several pairs, make each one a little different to prevent friends and family stealing each others' socks – and (if you are lucky) it will help you to pair them up every time you wash them!

Use a pure Jacob yarn, or a blend with mohair, which will be harder wearing and feel softer when worn (this is not a contradiction – the mohair is both smooth, so it feels softer, and hard-wearing).

YARN REQUIREMENTS
• Total amount of wool by weight and approximate length:

Walking Boot socks
Jacob/mohair or Jacob 4-ply
150 g/525 m (570 yds)

Welly Boot socks
Jacob/mohair or Jacob Aran
200 g/240 m (262 yds)

FINISHED SIZES

The instructions and quantities given are for a medium adult sock around 23 cm (9 in) long in the foot, which is about UK 6-8, EU 38-40 in shoe sizes, but the socks can be made to measure. The leg section of the walking boot socks is 20 cm (8 in), and 33 cm (13 in) for the rain boot version, which has only a small cuff turnover, but you can lengthen or shorten this to suit.

To adjust the foot, measure the length of the foot, subtract 10 cm (4 in) for the heel and toe parts, and the measurement you are left with gives you the middle length to knit. The rain boot socks fit snugly on a 38 cm (15 in) calf. If you need something larger, cast on additional stitches (refer to the tension to calculate the number needed) and then steadily reduce (over more rows than indicated) once you have completed the welt/turnover. Remember you will need more yarn if you do this.

SKILL LEVEL	

NEEDLES & NOTIONS

Walking Boot socks
1 set of four 2.75 mm (size 2) double pointed needles
1 set of four 3.25 mm (size 3) double pointed needles
Rain Boot socks
1 set of four 4 mm (size 6) double pointed needles
1 set of four 3.25 mm (size 3) double pointed needles

TENSION

Walking socks: 28 sts x 36 rows = 10 cm (4 in) square over main rib pattern
Rain Boot socks: 10 sts x 13 rows = 10 cm (4 in) square over stocking stitch
Adjust needle size to give required tension.

ABBREVIATIONS (see also page 140)

Stocking stitch: Normally one row k, one row p, but because you are knitting on three needles in turn, all sts will be k.
Graft off: Bind off the stitches together; use the third needle to help you.

Method

WALKING BOOT SOCKS (make 2)

Cast on 90 sts loosely using 3.25 mm (size 3) needles, with 30 sts on each of 3 needles and using Continental or long-tail cast-on. Change to 2.75 mm (size 2) needles and work 10 cm (4 in) in k1, p1, rib, (or k2, p1 if preferred). Change to 3.25 mm (size 3) needles and start rib pattern for leg: *k3, p2* and repeat from * to * until pattern section measures 20 cm (8 in). Next round: knit, decreasing evenly to 56 sts (19 on each of 2 needles and 18 on the third). Then work 9 rounds in stocking stitch (i.e. knit all stitches).

Divide for heel: k14, slip last 14 sts of round (from third needle) onto other end of the working needle, making 28 sts for heel and placing remaining 28 sts on two needles for instep.

Heel flap (knitted back and forth)

Row 1: sl 1 purlwise, purl to end.
Row 2: sl 1 purlwise with yarn behind, knit to end. Repeat until 17 rows have been worked.

Heel turn (knitted back and forth)

Row 1: k19, sl 1, k1, psso, turn.
Row 2: sl 1, p10, p2 tog, turn.
Row 3: sl 1, k10, sl 1, k1, psso, turn. Repeat Rows 2 and 3 five times, then row 2 once more.
Next row: sl 1, k to end, 14 sts remain.

Instep

Pick up and knit 13 sts along the right side, then knit the 28 sts left on the 2 needles for the instep, then knit 13 sts up left side to make 68 sts including the 14 from heel flap and continue in the round on 3 needles. Slip the last 7 sts from the last round on to the left hand needle. Then arrange stitches so there are 21 sts each on needles 1 and 3, 26 sts on needle 2.
Continue in stocking stitch:
Round 1: k19, k2tog, k26, sl 1, k1, psso, k19.
Round 2 and 3: knit.
Round 4: k18, k2tog, k26, sl 1, k1, psso, k18.
Repeat rows 1–4 3 times (56 sts), to make 15 sts on needles 1 and 3, and 26 sts on needle 2. Continue until desired foot length is reached, but remember the toe will make it about 5 cm (2 in) longer.

Shape toe

Round 1: k11, k2tog, k2, sl 1, k1, psso, k22, k2tog, k2, sl 1, k1, psso, k11.
Round 2 and every alternate round: knit.
Round 3: k10, k2tog, sl 1, k1, psso, k20, k2tog, k2, sl1, k1, psso, k10. Repeat these rounds, until 24 sts remain. Divide sts so you have 12 each on 2 needles and graft off, or finish using Kitchener stitch (see page 141).

RAIN BOOT SOCKS
(make 2)

Cast on 52 sts quite loosely, using 4 mm (size 6) needles, with 17 on the first 2 needles and 18 on the third, using Continental or long-tail cast-on. Change to 3.25 mm (size 3) needles.

Welt: work 10 cm (4 in) in rounds in k1, p1, rib, (or k3, p1 rib, as preferred – to use k2, p1 rib you need to reduce by 1 st and only cast on 51 sts), decreasing 1 st in last round to leave 51 sts. If you want a full turnover, make this section 20 cm (8 in) long.

Leg: next round: change to 4 mm needles, decrease by k2tog at beginning of round and k2togtbl at end of round. Then work 4 rounds in stocking stitch (i.e. knit all stitches). Repeat these 5 rounds twice (or more if you cast on more stitches), making 45 sts, then continue in stocking stitch to 33 cm (13 in) or the leg length required.

Divide for heel k11, slip last 12 sts of round onto same needle, making 23 sts for heel and placing remaining 22 sts on two needles for instep.

Heel flap (knitted back and forth)
Row 1: sl 1, purl to end.
Row 2: sl 1, knit to end.
Repeat until 9 more rows have been knitted, then make row 1 again (total 12 rows).

Heel turn (knitted back and forth)
Row 1: k13, sl 1, k1, psso, turn.
Row 2: p4, p2tog, turn.
Row 3: k5, sl 1, k1, psso, turn.
Row 4: p6, p2tog, turn.
Continue until all sts are on one needle.
Next row: k7, leave sts on left needle.

Instep
Slip instep sts onto one needle to give you a spare needle. Using the spare needle, k6, pick up and knit 12 sts from side of heel, then using a second needle knit across 22 instep sts, then using the third needle pick up and knit 11 sts along other side, k7, to make 58 sts.

Continue in stocking stitch:
Round 1: knit.
Round 2: first needle: knit to last 3 sts, k2tog, k1, second needle: knit, third needle: k1, k2tog tbl, knit to end.
Repeat rounds 1–2 until 44 sts remain (14 rounds in total). Then continue until desired foot length is reached: but remember this is the foot, with heel in place so allow for the toe which will make it about 5 cm (2 in) longer.

REINFORCING HEELS AND TOES

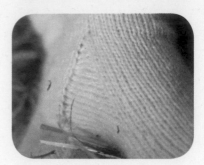

Some people wear out their heels, some their toes, and some both! There are three ways to reinforce heels and toes:

• Add a strand of finer yarn (a strong sewing cotton or nylon thread works well) as you work the heel.

• Darn through the stitches after completing the sock.

• Try heel stitch, which is worked over two rows.
Row 1: right side facing [*sl 1 purlwise, k1* repeat to end].
Row 2: [sl 1 purlwise, purl to end]. This makes a subtle ribbed effect and a denser fabric (it will also help you to count your heel flap rows as each of the slipped stitches represents two worked rows).

Shape toe
Row 1: first needle: k to last 3 sts, k2tog, k1, second needle: k1, k2tog tbl, k to last 3 sts, k2tog, k1, third needle: k1, k2tog tbl, k to end.
Row 2: knit.
Repeat these rows 4 times until 24 sts remain.
Split the 24 sts into 12 on each of 2 needles and graft off, or finish using Kitchener stitch (see page 141).

Manx Loaghtan fleece

The first thing that you notice about Manx Loaghtan sheep is their impressive sets of horns. Some rams and ewes have four horns, while others have six, two, or, in the case of some ewes, none at all. Being active, the sheep can bend or break their horns, so a beautiful symmetrical set is somewhat rare. They are known to have grazed the hills of the Isle of Man since the 11th century.

The Manx Loaghtan are small brown sheep, although they bleach to cream in the sun. The lambs are born black and gradually achieve their particular shade of brown during the first year. (It is possible to keep Manx Loaghtan sheep from bleaching by keeping them indoors and letting them graze by moonlight.)

However, as with most primitive sheep, there is a wide variety of shades of brown, usually getting paler, with more kemp fibres, with age. It is possible that differences in soil on the island cause fleeces to be darker brown in the north than in the south, although there may be a genetic reason for this.

They have long hairless legs and are lean, though selective breeding for meat has meant some are now larger and more solidly built. Normally ewes weigh around 35 kg (77 lbs) and rams 45 kg (99 lbs).

Living on a small island has inevitably tended to make these sheep rare, and they are classified as At Risk by the Rare Breeds Survival Trust, with fewer than 1,500 registered breeding ewes.

Manx Loaghtan meat from the Isle of Man gained Protected Designation of Origin from the European Community in 2009.

The breed is believed to be the closest relative of the extinct Jersey sheep. A flock now grazes there and supplies fleeces for a 5-ply Guernsey yarn used for the traditional local pullovers.

BREED AT A GLANCE

Sheep type: Primitive.

Appearance: Small, brown sheep with two, four or six horns.

Rare breeds status: Classified 'At Risk' by the UK Rare Breeds Survival Trust. A conservation breed in the US.

Further information: UK breed society: www.manxLoaghtansheep.org.

History: Originally from the Isle of Man, off the west coast of the UK. Their name in Manx, *lugh dhoan*, means mouse-brown. Although considered native to the Isle of Man, they are part of the northern short-tail family of primitive sheep also found in Scotland and Wales.

DK yarn

FLEECE FACT FILE

Fleece weight: 1.5–2 kg (3–5 lbs)
Staple length: 7–10 cm (2.5–4 in). A shearling might produce longer wool, perhaps up to 12 cm (4.75 in)
Micron count: Around 30
Crimp: Indistinct
Handle: Soft/medium
Natural colours: Nut-brown; may bleach to cream in the sun
Mixed colours: None
Lustre: None

raw fleece

carded pure
Manx fleece

Aran yarn

Close-up of pure DK knitted sample.

carded
Hebridean/Manx
blend yarn

4-ply yarn

Manx Loaghtan yarn

Manx Loaghtan yarn is known for its unusual brown 'moorit' colour – some fleeces are fine and fluffy, but others are distinctly hairy and coarser. It knits into a lightweight but warm fabric, and is also good for weaving into heavier items.

The raw wool is quite short, with no lustre and an indistinct crimp but good resilience and bulk. The best examples will happily make 4-ply yarns, but the majority of fleeces are more suitable for Double Knitting, Aran or Chunky yarns.

The bulkiness makes for light, warm garments. With these properties in mind, we have chosen a scarf, hat and mittens pattern, but the yarn will work well for the Black Welsh Mountain, Castlemilk Moorit, Hebridean, Herdwick, Jacob, North Ronaldsay and Zwartbles designs.

The wool is hard-wearing and works well for woven tweeds, tartans, rugs and blankets. It adds a contrast with naturally coloured stripes and checks in white fabrics.

However, Manx Loaghtan fleece can be bitty and gives low yields when spun commercially. It is easier to

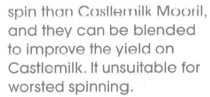

YARN USER'S GUIDE

Good for ...
- Hard-wearing, lightweight garments
- Sweaters and socks
- Blankets and rugs
- Blending
- Dyeing when blended
- Bulk, loft

Not so good for ...
- Garments worn next to the skin
- Baby clothes
- Drape

spin than Castlemilk Moorit, and they can be blended to improve the yield on Castlemilk. It unsuitable for worsted spinning.

Manx Loaghtan blends well with Hebridean to make a rich brown yarn with greater depth of colour than the mid-brown alone, which can be dull if bleached fibre is included. It also works well with mohair to make a softer yarn in a pale coffee shade, which will dye to strawberry or golden hues. With mohair, it is possible to make a semi-worsted yarn.

Manx Loaghtan is ideal for sweaters and jackets. The results are hard-wearing, lightweight and firrm to the touch.

Zig-zag scarf, hat and mittens

By Sue Blacker

The zig-zag texture for this hat and scarf set is easy to follow as it is a combination of knit and purl stitches. They are fully reversible. For the set, with its stocking stitch mittens, I have chosen rich brown Manx Loagthan as it's such a lovely warming colour, and the Double Knitting yarn gives density and warmth. They could be made for all the family in a range of rare breeds (can you suit the breed to the person?).

To keep the scarf and mittens together, add buttons to the ends of the scarf and buttonholes or loops to the mittens so they can be buttoned together.

The mittens are knitted in the round, but two needles can be used (instructions are given for this in brackets where appropriate).

Method

Twisted rib panel
For mittens over 7 sts
Row 1: p1, k2, p1, k2, p1.
Rows 2, 3, 4, 5 and **6:** as row 1 if knitting in the round (but if using two needles, rows 2, 4 and 6, k1 p2 k1 p2 k1).
Row 7: p1, Tw2, p1, Tw2, p1.
Row 8: as row 1 (as row 2).

Shallow Zig-zag pattern
For Beanie Hat over 12 rows, multiples of 6sts.
The chart on page 94 shows the design over 39 sts. RS rows are worked from right to left, and WS from left to right. The last 4 rows reverse some from the first 8. Written instructions are below.

Deep Zig-zag design
For scarf over 48 rows, multiple of 6 sts plus 3.
The chart on page 94 shows the design and moss stitch edges. The second 24 rows reverse the first 24. Written instructions are also provided below.

YARN REQUIREMENTS

Manx Loagthan Double Knitting yarn
• Total amount of wool by weight and approximate length:
Adult scarf:
250 g/550 m (595 yds)
Child's scarf:
200 g/440 m (476 yds)
Beanie hat:
100 g/220 m (238 yds)
Adult Mittens:
(all sizes):
100 g/220 m (238 yds)
Child's mittens:
(both sizes):
50 g/110 m (119 yds)

SCARF

Using 4.5 mm (size 7) needles, cast on 47 stitches for adult's scarf or 35 sts for child's scarf.

Base edge: rows 1 and 2: garter st (knit all sts)

Now start the Deep Zig-zag Design, with 3st moss st border at each side, slipping the first st and knitting the last st of every row to make an even edge:

Row 1: sl1, p1, k1, p1, (p3, k3) to last 7 sts, k3, p1, k1, p1, k1.
Row 2: sl1, k1, p1, k1, (p3, k3) to last 7 sts, p3, k1, p1, k2.
Row 3: as row 1.
Row 4: as row 2.
Row 5: sl1, p1, k1, p2, (k3, p3) to last 6 sts, k2, p1, k1, p1, k1.
Row 6: sl1, k1, p1, k1, p2, (k3, p3) to last 5 sts, k2, p1, k2.
Row 7: as row 5.
Row 8: as row 6.
Row 9: sl1, p1, k1, p2 (k3, p3) to last 5 sts, k2, p1, k2.
Row 10, sl1, k1, p1, k1 (k3, p3) to last 6 sts, k3, p1, k2.
Row 11: as row 9.
Row 12: as row 10.
Row 13: sl1, p1, k1, p4 (k3, p3) to last 4 sts, p1, k1, p1, k1.
Row 14: sl1, k1, p1, k4 (p3, k3) to last 4 sts, k1, p1, k2.
Row 15: as row 13.
Row 16: as row 14.
Row 17: sl1, p1, k1, p1, (p3, k3) to last 7 sts, p3, k1, p1, k1.
Row 18: sl1, k1, p1, k3 (p3, k3) to last 5 sts, p1, k1, p1, k2.
Row 19: as row 17.
Row 20: as row 18.
Row 21: sl1, p1, k1, p1, k2 (p3, k3) to last 5 sts, p2, k1, p1, k1.
Row 22: sl1, k1, p1, k2 (p3, k3) to last 6 sts, p2, k1, p1, k2.
Row 23: as row 21.
Row 24: as row 22.
Row 25: as row 1.
Row 26: as row 2.
Row 27: as row 1.
Row 28: as row 2.
Row 29: as row 21.
Row 30: as row 22.
Row 31: as row 21.
Row 32: as row 22.

Row 33: as row 17.
Row 34: as row 18.
Row 35: as row 17.
Row 36: as row 18.
Row 37: as row 13.
Row 38: as row 14.
Row 39: as row 13.
Row 40: as row 14.
Row 41: as row 9.
Row 42: as row 10.
Row 43: as row 9.
Row 44: as row 10.
Row 45: as row 5.
Row 46: as row 6.
Row 47: as row 5.
Row 48: as row 6.

Work in pattern until required length, finishing with 2 rows of garter stitch. There is no need to complete a set of 48 rows. However with complete repeats scarf design will be the same at each end. Cast off.

MEASUREMENTS

Adult scarf: 183 cm (72 in) long, 25.5 cm (10 in) wide
Child's scarf: 130 cm (51 in) long, 18 cm (7 in) wide
Beanie hat: made to measure, see below
Adult mittens (around hand): 17 (19, 21) cm (6.75 (7.5, 8.25) in)
Child's mittens (around hand): 13.5 (15.5) cm (5.5 (6) in)
Instructions are given for smallest size first, followed by medium and large in brackets. If only one is given, it applies to all sizes.

NEEDLES & NOTIONS
Scarf: one pair 4.5 mm (size 7) knitting needles
Beanie: one pair 4 mm (size 6) knitting needles (or 4.5 mm (size 7) circular needle if preferred)
Mittens: one set of 4 DPN 3.25 mm (size 3) knitting needles, at least 20 cm (8 in) long and one set of 4 DPN 3.25 mm (size 3) knitting needles 12.5 cm (5 in) long (If knitting on two needles)
1 pair of 3.25 mm (size 3) needles)
2 buttons (wood or horn work well with Manx)
Stitch holders
Stitch marker (if knitting in the round)
Crochet hook

TENSION
Approx 19 sts x 24 rows = 10 cm (4 in) over stocking stitch on 4.5 mm (size 7) needles
Adjust needle size to give required tension.

ABBREVIATIONS
See Knitting Know-How (page 140)

Tassel fringe
Wind yarn around a piece of card 8 cm (3 in) wide and cut along one edge to make short threads. Using a crochet hook, and with each thread folded in half, insert hook into sts along end of scarf, pull through looped part of thread and pull ends through loop. You will need around half as many threads as stitches, depending on desired density of the fringe.

CHILDREN'S MITTENS
Using 3.25 mm (size 3) needles, cast on 36 (40) sts and work 18 rows of k1, p1 rib, then 2 rows of stocking stitch.
If you wish to button the mittens to the scarf, use two needles and leave a gap in the seam to act as the buttonhole.

Right mitten

Set up row: k6 (7) p1, k2, p1, k2, p1, k to end. Next row k (p) maintaining rib (see page 90).

Thumb

Row 1: k17 (19) m1, k2, m1, k17 (19). Work 3 rows stocking stitch after each increase row.
Row 5: k17 (19) m1, k4, m1, k17 (19).
Row 9: k17 (19) m1, k6, m1, k17 (19).
Row 13: k17 (19) m1, k8 m1, k17 (19).
Work 1 (3) rows stocking stitch.

Next row: k27 (29) turn, cast on 1 (2) sts and leave remaining sts on needle (st holder). Change to 5 in (12.5 cm) DPN.
Next row: p11 (12) turn, cast on 1 (2) sts, leave remaining sts on needles (st holder) work 3.75 (4.5) cm (1.5 (1.75) in) on 12 (14) sts (end with p row).

Shape thumb

Row 1: * k1, k2tog, rep from * to end (to last 2 sts k2).
Row 2: k (p).
Row 3: k2tog to end.
Break yarn, thread through sts and fasten off (sew seam).

Hand

Right side facing rejoin yarn, pick up and k 2 (4) sts from base of thumb then k to end of round (row). 36 (42) sts. Continue in st st and rib until hand measures 6.5 (7.5) cm (2.5 (3) in) from base of thumb.

Shape top

Row 1: k1, k2tog tbl, pattern 12 (15) k2tog, k2, k2tog tbl, pattern 12 (15) k2tog, k1.
Row 2: knit (purl) and all alt rounds (rows).
Row 3: k1, k2tog tbl, pattern 10 (13) k2tog, k2, k2tog tbl, pattern 10 (13) k2tog, k1.
Continue to dec in this way until 20 (26) sts are left.
Work one more row.
Turn mitten inside out, divide sts in half and place on two needles. Graft together or work a three-needle cast off (cast off and sew side seam).

Left mitten

Work as for right mitten except for pattern set up row: k23 (26) p1, k2, p1, k2, p1, k6 (7).
Next row knit (purl).

ADULT MITTENS

There are three sizes and may be worked entirely in stocking stitch or with twisted rib panels on the back of the hand. Work in the round or on two needles (instructions are given in square brackets where different).

Right mitten

Cast on 40 (44, 48) sts on 3.25 mm (size 3) DPN needles divided as follows 15 – 10 – 15 (16 – 12 – 16, 16 – 16 – 16) (or use two needles) and work in k2, p2, rib for 26 rows.
Large size only: work 2 rows st st.
Pattern set up row: large size only k10, p1, k2, p1, k2, p1, k to end. Next row knit (purl).
Set up row for small and medium sizes and start of thumb shaping for all sizes:

Shallow zig-zag pattern for hat (12 rows, multiples of 6 plus 3 sts)

Shallow zig-zag pattern for scarf (48 rows, multiples of 6 plus 3 sts)

LEGEND

☐ k on RS; p on WS   ☐ p on RS; k on WS

Row 1: k8 (8, 10) p1, k2, p1, k2, p1, k4, (6, 6) m1, k2, m1, k19 (21, 23).
Continue Twisted Rib pattern and work 3 rows st st after this and following increase rows.

Shape for thumb
Row 1: k19 (21, 23) m1, k2, m1, k19 (21, 23). Work 3 rows in st st after this row and each of the following increase rows.
Row 5: k19 (21, 23) m1, k4, m1, k19 (21, 23).
Row 9: K19 (21, 23) m1, k6, m1, k19 (21, 23).
Row 13: k19 (21, 23) m1, k8 m1, k19 (21, 23).
Row 17: k19 (21, 23) m1, k10, m1, k19 (21, 23).

Small and medium sizes only work one row.
Large Size only:
Row 21: k23, m1, k12, m1, k23.
Row 22: knit (purl). This completes thumb shaping.

Thumb
Row 1: k31 (33, 37) turn cast on 1 (2, 2) sts.
Row 2: p13, (14, 16) turn cast on 1 (2, 2).
Using hort DPNs divide these 14 (16, 18) sts between 3 needles: 5 – 4 – 5 (5 – 6 – 5, 6 – 6 – 6) and work in st st for 2 (2.25, 2.5)in (5.5 (6, 6.5) cm).
Shape top of thumb
Row 1: * k1, k2tog, rep from * to last 2 sts k2 (to the last st k1: to end).
Row 2: knit 1 round (purl 1 row).
Row 3: k2tog 5 times (k2tog 5 times k1, k2tog 6 times) Break yarn leaving a tail, thread through the remaining sts and fasten off (sew thumb seam).

Hand
Right side facing, rejoin yarn to sts on right hand needle. Pick up and k 6 (4, 6) sts along base of thumb, then k sts on left hand needle. 44 (46, 52) sts.
Work 1.75 (1.75, 2) in (4.5 (4.5 5) cm) in st st (end with purl row).

Continue, keeping pattern as set and working thumb, until hand measures 10 (11, 12) cm (4 (4.25, 4.75) in) from base of thumb.

Shape top
Row 1: k1, k2tog tbl, pattern 16 (17, 20) k2tog, k2, k2tog tbl, pattern 16 (17, 20) k2tog, k1.
Row 2 and all alt rows: knit (purl) keeping pattern correct.
Row 3: k1, k2tog tbl, pat 14 (15, 18) k2tog, k2, k2tog tbl, pat 14 (15, 18) k2tog, k1.
Continue to decrease in this way until 28 (30, 36) sts are left. Work one more row.
Divide these sts in half and place on two needles then graft together or work a three needle cast off (cast off and sew up seam).

Left mitten
Work as for right mitten except for pattern set up row:
Large Size only: K31, p1, k2, p1, k2, p1, k10.
Next row knit (purl).
Small and medium sizes and the start of thumb shaping for all sizes:
Row 1: k19 (21: 23), m1, k2, m1, k4 (6, 6), p1, k2, p1, k2, p1, k8 (8, 10).
Continue as right mitten.

BEANIE HAT
Making to measure
Measure the circumference of the head, including the ears, for which you are making the hat, or copy the size of an existing one. Add 5 cm (2 in) to your measurement to give the total width. For example, if the head is 60 cm (23.5 in) your knitting will be 65 cm (25.5 in) wide. For the length, measure from the ear lobes to the middle of the head. For the length to knit, add 8 cm (3 in) to allow for a turn over at the brim. (For a child's size, add 5 cm (2 in).) Omit turnover if you prefer.

Pattern
Using 4 mm (size 6) needles, cast on 10 sts loosely for every 5 cm (2 in) of calculated width (e.g. if width is 60 cm (24 in), cast on 120 sts). This pattern requires an even number of sts, and multiples of 3 sts, so add extra to make this work (e.g. for 55 cm (21.5 in), which needs 110 sts, make it 114, etc.).

Work Shallow Zig-zag pattern as on chart opposite or as below.
Row 1: (k3, p3) to end.
Row 2: as round/row 1.
Row 3: p1 (k3, p3) to last 2 sts, p2.
Row 4: as round/row 3.
Row 5: p2, (k3, p3) to last st, p1.
Row 6: as round/row 5.
Row 7: (p3, k3) to end.
Row 8: as round/row 7.
Row 9: as row 5.
Row 10: as row 5.
Row 11: as row 3.
Row 12: as row 3.
Continue in pattern until work measures the required length, less 8 cm (3 in) for crown.

Shape crown
Row 1: (k1, k2tog, p1, p2 tog) all round, reducing sts by one third. Now continue in the Shallow Zig-zag pattern, but only 2 sts wide:
Row 2: (k2, p2) to end.
Row 3: p1, (k2, p2) to last 2 sts, p2.
Row 4: as row/round 3.
Row 5: (p2, K2) to end.
Row 6: as row/round 5.
Row 7: as row/round 3.
Row 8: as row/round 4.
Continue with 2 sts-wide zig-zag pattern until required length. To help close the centre, reduce number of sts by working k2tog, p2tog across the last row.

Break off yarn, leaving a long thread. Use darning needle to thread through all sts and pull tightly to gather. Fasten securely. Sew side seam. Oversew gap at crown or cover with a pom-pom (see page 141).

North Ronaldsay fleece

The multicoloured North Ronaldsay – single sheep and entire flocks vary from white to dark grey, as well as moorit browns – have strong personalities. They tend to scatter, rather than cluster, when threatened and have scant respect for dogs or people. They are (marginally!) easier to manage with a bucket of feed.

As they are so small, with neither rams nor ewes generally exceeding 30 kg (66 lbs), North Ronaldsay sheep have been mainly kept for wool rather than meat. Their fleeces are almost a double coat, like cashmere goats or Icelandic sheep. This means there is a short soft undercoat mixed with a longer, hair coat.

Research suggests today's sheep are little changed from the 'original' type, with similar skeletons found on the island of North Ronaldsay in Stone Age settlements.

These sheep are suited to conservation grazing, as they will browse from grass, but also hedges, bushes and woody plants. It is great to watch these little sheep carefully picking gorse, thistle or bramble flowers without pricking their lips.

North Ronaldsay sheep also eat seaweed – useful on islands where grass is sparse and there are few trees. Indeed, since 1832 the North Ronaldsay flock has been confined to the island foreshore by a 1.8-metre (6-foot) high dry-stone wall for almost all the year.

Of course, this is a rare breed, classified as Endangered by the Rare Breeds Survival Trust, with less than 500 registered breeding ewes. However, the breed society, which was only established in 1997, has helped to popularise North Ronaldsay sheep and there are now flocks throughout the UK. On the island, the flock manages itself: only those able to withstand the local conditions can survive and breed.

BREED AT A GLANCE

Sheep type: Primitive. Northern, short-tailed.
Appearance: Small, multicoloured sheep, both within single sheep and across the flock, ranging from white to dark grey and also browns and fawns. They have neat curling horns on all rams and a few ewes, and hair-less legs.
Rare breeds status: Rare Breeds Survival Trust classification is Endangered.
Further information: UK breed society: www.nrsf.co.uk.
History: Farmed on the Orkney Islands off the north of Scotland for centuries; thought to have been established in the UK around the 9th century, probably by mixing sheep brought by Viking and Saxon raiders with the local (and most likely very similar) sheep.

White DK yarn

mid-grey Aran yarn

FLEECE FACT FILE
Fleece weight: 1.5–2 kg (3–4 lbs), but often nearer 1 kg (2 lbs)
Staple length: 4–8 cm (1.5–3 in)
Micron count: 25–40
Crimp: Variable, coarse
Handle: Fine with some kemp
Natural colours: White, pale to dark grey, browns and fawns
Mixed colours: Greys
Lustre: Slight

White Aran yarn

dark grey DK yarn

Close-up of knitted Aran sample

raw fleece

dark grey Aran yarn

scoured fleece

carded fleece

North Ronaldsay yarn

In common with Icelandic sheep and cashmere goats, North Ronaldsay sheep have a double coat – a short, soft undercoat mixed with a longer, hair coat. The proportion of soft fibres enables North Ronaldsay yarns to feel much softer than the numbers imply.

In cashmere, it is necessary to remove the coarser hair before spinning the fleece, but doing this with North Ronaldsay, in my view, completely removes the character of the fleece, as the hairs are usually dark and white and add more natural colour to the yarns.

These yarns come up naturally quite strongly heathered and can be sorted into shades of white, pale grey, dark grey and brown-grey for spinning. Scouring requires the removal of salt and sand, not common with other sheep!

Owing to the character of the fleece, it works best in thicker yarns, from Double Knitting upwards. It can be over-dyed and felted, but I feel it is too rare for this and prefer to make naturally coloured yarns.

The yarns, like the wool, are designed to have structure, lightness and bulk, making ideal warm layers, so we have chosen an airy waistcoat in Aran-weight yarn as a pattern.

YARN USER'S GUIDE
Good for ...
- Spinning
- Felting
- Dyeing
- Weaving

Not so good for ...
- Fine yarns

Due to the multi-coloured and heathered nature of the yarn, it does not work as well as more monochrome yarns to show distinct texture in cables or other textured designs. However, North Ronaldsay yarn would also work for the Black Welsh Mountain waistcoat, the Manx Loagthan scarf, mittens and hat, the Hebridean cushion cover, the Zwartbles cardigan or, combined with other dyed yarns, a version of the Shetland waistcoat. It can also be used for blankets made from squares knitted using different colours.

Paler North Ronaldsay fleeces can be dyed successfully. As it is produced by hardy sheep it is perhaps not surprising that the wool is best used for warm, durable outer garments.

Airy waistcoat

By Myra Mortlock

This smart casual waistcoat comes in two sizes and is worked in three pieces, then joined at the shoulders. It is trimmed with a stylish curled edge at the armholes and neck before finally joining the side seams. The pattern has a garter and moss-stitch panel design and is light and airy to give more warmth. For a more formal and lacier style, knit in Double Knitting worsted-spun yarn, increasing needle size for tension.

The waistcoat is closed with a toggle or button, but you could use a brooch or shawl pin instead.

Method

BACK

With 6.5 mm (size 10.5) knitting needles, cast on 63 69 sts.
Row 1: (k3, p3) repeat to last 3 sts, k3.
Row 2: (k3, p1, k1, p1) repeat to last 3 sts, k3.
Repeat Row 2 to form pattern. Continue until work measures 26 (28) cm (10.25 (11) in).

Shape armhole
Tip: Slip 1st st of every decrease row to give smooth curve.
Row 1: cast off 3 sts at start of row; work in pattern to end.
Row 2: as row 1.
Row 3: cast off 2 sts at start of row; work in pattern to end.
Row 4: as row 3.
Row 5: cast off 1 st at start of row; work in pattern to end.
Row 6: as row 5.
Work 2 more rows without decreasing.

YARN REQUIREMENTS
North Ronaldsay Aran yarn
• Total amount of wool by weight and approximate length:
UK size 12-14: 350 g/490 m (532 yd)
UK size 16-18: 400 g/560 m (608 yd)

K 2 together at beginning and end of next row.
Repeat these 3 rows twice.
Work 3 rows without shaping.
K 2 tog at beginning and end of next row 43 (49) sts remain.
Continue until work measures 47 (51) cm (18.5 (20) in).

Shape back neck
Work 15 (17) sts and turn.
Next row: at neck edge k2 tog, work to armhole end.

Shape shoulder
Cast off 7 (8) sts. Work return row without shaping.
Cast off remaining sts. Leave centre 13 (15) sts on a holder.
Finish other shoulder to match.

FRONTS (make 2)
NOTE: the side seams are offset towards the back, and there is an extra five-stitch decrease on each front underarm.

With 6.5 mm (size 10.5) needles, cast on 36 (39) sts.
Row 1: Smaller size (k3, p3) repeat to end. Larger size (p3, k3) repeat to last 3 sts, p3.
Row 2: Both sizes (p1, k1, p1, k3) repeat to end, larger size, last 3 sts, p1, k1, p1.
Form pattern by repeating garter st and moss st panels as for back.
Continue until piece measures 21 (22) cm (8.25 (8.5) in).

Shape centre front opening
(Small size has K3 at centre edge of both fronts).
Row 1: Cast off 4 sts; pattern to end.
Row 2: (also row 4, 6 and 8) work without shaping.
Row 3: Cast off 3 sts; work in pattern to end.
Row 5: Cast off 2 sts; work in pattern to end.
Row 7: Cast off 1 st; pattern to end.
Row 9: Cast off 1 st, pattern to end.

SMALL SIZE: at armhole edge cast off 5 sts.
Keeping front edge straight, on next alternate row cast off 3 sts at underarm; following alternate row 2 sts; next alternate row 1 st. Work in pattern on 14 sts until work measures 47 cm (18.5 in).
Cast off 7 sts at shoulder edge.
Work one row without shaping.
Cast off remaining sts

LARGE SIZE: continue until piece measures 28 cm (11 in).
At armhole edge cast off 5 sts. On next alternate row cast off 3 sts at underarm, following alternate row 2 sts; next alternate row 1 st; next alternate row 1 st. Work in pattern on 16 sts until work measures same as back to shoulder. Cast off 8sts at armhole. Work 1 row. Cast off remaining 6 sts.

Work second front, laying the pieces side by side to check they are a mirror image as you work. Join shoulder seams.

Work armhole facings
RS facing pick up 37 (41) sts from Front underarm to shoulder and 32 (37) sts from shoulder seam to Back underarm. 69 (78) sts.

MEASUREMENTS
Garment bust size: 102 (112) cm (40 (44) in)
Length from base to back neck: 47 (51) cm (18.5 (20) in)
Instructions are given for the smallest size first, followed by large in brackets

NEEDLES & NOTIONS
1 pair 6.5 mm (size 10.5) knitting needles
1 large toggle or decorative button
1 stitch holder or spare knitting needle

TENSION
Approx 13.5 sts x 10 rows = 10 cm (4 in) over stocking stitch on 6.5 mm (size 10.5) needles
Adjust needle size to give required tension.

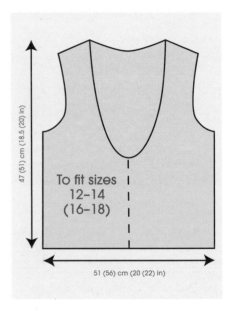

47 (51) cm (18.5 (20) in)

To fit sizes
12–14
(16–18)

51 (56) cm (20 (22) in)

WS facing: purl. RS facing: knit. Cast off loosely.

Neck and front facing
RS facing, pick up 37 sts from front edge to shoulder seam, 2 sts from back shaping, 15 sts from holder, 2 sts from other side back shaping and 37 sts to other front edge. 93 sts.
WS facing: purl. RS facing: knit. Cast off loosely.
Make thread loop and sew on button. Place garment on a cloth, press to shape and cover with a damp cloth. When almost dry transfer to a hanger to allow facings to set.

Romney fleece

The Romney adapted to survive on exposed and isolated salt marshes. This has served them well and they are found across the world – from Portugal to North and South America and the Falkland Islands, New Zealand and Australia. The UK breed society claims: 'The sun never sets on Romney sheep'.

The Romney sheep has a large, dense, versatile, longwool fleece with a range of fibre types, from coarse to fine, which differ according to where the animal was bred. For example, the UK micron count is 30–34 on average, but more like 35–37 microns in New Zealand and half-way between these two in the US.

The Romney has travelled the world as a pure-bred animal and to crossbreed and create the Perendale, Driesdale, Coopworth and Corriedale breeds. In New Zealand they supplanted the Merinos to number half the total sheep in the country by the 1850s, rising to three-quarters by 1955. They became the basis of the country's lamb meat trade. The Romney was first imported to the US in 1904.

At present, New Zealand Romneys are being imported into the UK to use as terminal sires for meat breeding. Ewes weigh from 65–85 kg (143–187 lbs) and rams from 90–110 kg (198–242 lbs).

As you might expect, the Romney is not rare, but it comes in many forms. For example, the fleece may be very fine and evenly crimped, or considerably coarser with an indistinct crimp. Although they are generally white, some can be black or brown. There is a flock in southern England, attached to a small worsted-spinning mill, which has Black Romneys, bred pure over several generations.

BREED AT A GLANCE

Sheep type: Medieval longwool.

Appearance: Perhaps the classic medium-large white sheep from children's picture books! The Romney has a bulky, mid-length white semi-lustre fleece, no horns, a top-knot, forward pointing ears set on the side of the head and a fat, long tail.

Rare breeds status: None.

Further information:
UK breed society: www.romneysheepuk.com.
US and Canada breed society: www.americanromney.org.

History: Has grazed the low-lying Romney Marsh in Kent, southeast England, for centuries. They probably gained some genes from Roman imports, but the modern sheep originate from the 13th century, although they were 'improved' with some Leicester genes in the 18th century.

raw fleece

scoured
fleece

FLEECE FACT FILE
Fleece weight: 3–5 kg (7–11 lbs)
Staple length: 10–17 cm (4–7 in)
Micron count: UK average: 30–34, New
Zealand average 35–57, US average 30–35
Crimp: Well-defined
Handle: Coarse to fine
Natural colours: White, black, brown
Mixed colours: Browns and greys
Lustre: Semi-lustre

carded fleece

Close-up of knitted Guernsey sample

5 ply Guernsey
yarn

Romney yarn

The considerable variations in Romney yarns – we have found wool as fine and soft as Corriedale, but with the added lustre – mean it can be used for many things. While it is ideal for hard-wearing items such as gloves, socks and jackets, softer wool can be used for garments worn next to the skin. Coarser examples should be used for durable rugs, mats and chair seats.

The majority of New Zealand Romney wool is used for carpets, providing the bulk and resilience to go with the harder wearing attributes of mountain sheep such as Driesdale in New Zealand or Cheviot and Welsh Mountain in the UK.

The wool is good for hand-spinning and quite easy for beginners, with relatively low lanolin, so it is also easier to wash and has a higher yield than others wools.

We have used a mixed range of British Romney wool to make a 5-ply Guernsey yarn and have also used Romney to make a grey/fawn version of this yarn, blended with Hebridean and Manx Loagthan wool.

Careful selection would enable Romney wool to work from Double Knitting to Chunky yarns and provide soft, bulky warm results, with softer, finer fibre best suited to woollen spinning and the more mixed and coarser fibre better worsted-spun.

Since we are using a 5-ply Guernsey yarn, which is also relatively inelastic and so will not knit up as economically as woollen-spun yarns, the obvious choice is our Guernsey design.

However, these 5-ply yarns can also be used for textured designs on bags, Aran designs (use large needles to make it go further), accessories (use the yarn with three or four strands at a time for the Herdwick designs) or pillows, and could also be considered for socks as this yarn is also hard wearing.

YARN USER'S GUIDE

Good for ...
- Carpets
- Inner or outer garments, depending on the fleece
- Rugs, mats and pillows
- Dyeing
- Hand-spinning
- Felting

Not so good for ...
- Baby clothes

Romney yarns are ideal for textured knits and this, combined with the resilience of the fibres, makes it ideal for the Guernsey pattern.

Traditional Guernsey pullover

By Sue Blacker

A Guernsey is a traditional sweater worn by fishermen. I have chosen a white Romney yarn because it is probably the easiest to work with for a first-time Guernsey knitter. And, although I have not found any examples, I believe the fishermen of Kent would have worn Guernseys like those from Cornwall, Guernsey, Jersey, Yorkshire, Wales, Ireland or Scotland.

This is a traditionally knitted and styled Guernsey. They are normally quite close fitting so if you want it loose, make a larger size! However, it is relatively easy to resize Guernseys, and instructions are given for this within the pattern.

The body is worked in the round, then back and forth for the yoke, with the sleeves also knitted in the round, picking up and working downwards from the shoulders, and again finished with a deep rib welt.

Two designs are given for the yoke, one plainer and one more detailed, but you can always continue in stocking stitch (at the risk of terminal boredom?).

Make a traditional submariner's pullover by knitting the garment entirely in stocking stitch and making a polo neck.

YARN REQUIREMENTS

White Romney 5-ply Guernsey Knitting yarn
• Total amount of wool by weight and approximate length:
Small: 800 g/1,856 m (1,936 yds)
Medium: 900 g/2,080 m (2,178 yds)
Large: 1,000 g/2,320 m (2,420 yds)

Method

BODY (make 1)

Using 2.25 mm (size 1) circular needle, and English/long-tail method, cast on 336 (372, 408) sts. Ensuring the sts are not twisted, join into a round. Work k3, p3 rib for 8 cm (3 in) (or less or more, as preferred).

Increase by 12 sts evenly around the last round to make 348 (384, 420) sts, finishing in line with the cast-on tail.

Mark the side seam lines by purling 1 st at each side of work on each round:
Mark the next st as one side and count around 173 (191, 209) sts to the other side to

make the second mark, so you have 2 sides of 173 (191, 209) sts each, plus 2 seam sts.

Tip: You can make these lines as garter stitch by working one knit and one purl stitch on alternate rounds, so they will show less – but this is more to remember!

Continue in st st (all rounds k sts) until the work measures 36 cm (14 in) (or longer or shorter as preferred).

Begin pattern and gussets
See pages 106–107 for pattern.
Do not start gussets until you have decided on your pattern.

GUSSETS

The gussets are worked in st st, starting from the side seams and increasing by 2 sts on each gusset, and at each edge of the growing gusset every 4th row. The first increase is made by working into both sides of the seam stitch to make 3 sts from one. Continue the increases for 48 rows to make each gusset 25 sts wide plus 2 seam stitches. The new stitches become seam stitches on either side of the gusset and can be worked in purl or garter stitch to maintain the line. You can include them in the pattern as their position is obvious at this stage. However, once the sleeve has been added there will be a seam stitch to mark where decreases are made on either side, so for the first-time Guernsey knitter, it is worth continuing with seam stitches.

Once you have worked 48 gusset rows the work will measure about 46 cm (18 in) from the cast-on edge, making the gusset about 12.5 cm (5 in) long to its widest point, and the front and back will each still consist of 173 (191, 209) sts.

MEASUREMENTS
Chest: 92 (102, 112) cm (36 (40, 44) in)
Actual chest: 112 (128, 142) cm (44 (50, 54) in)
Length from shoulder to hem: 69 cm (27 in)
Length from under-arm gussets to hem: 36 cm (14 in)
Yoke length: 33 cm (13 in)
Sleeve seam: 48 cm (19 in)
Instructions are given for the smallest size first, followed by medium and large in brackets).

SKILL LEVEL	🧶🧶🧶

NEEDLES & NOTIONS
1 pair 2.25 mm (size 1) long, straight needles
1 pair 2.25 mm (size 1) 39 in (100 cm) circular needle
1 set of four 2.25 mm (size 1) double-pointed needles (for narrow section of sleeve)
Cable needle
Stitch markers or coloured thread
2 stitch holders or waste yarn

TENSION
Approx 36 sts x 40 rows = 10 cm (4 in) over stocking stitch on 2.25 mm (size 1) needles.
Adjust needle size to give required tension.
A simple way to increase the size of the garment is to increase the needle size, although this will also reduce the stitch density and therefore the wind-proof characteristics of the final garment (but check your tension if you plan to do this).
Using 2.75 mm (size 2) needles will give approximately 34 sts and 39 rows to 10 cm (4 in) and add approximately 18 cm (7 in) to the chest size.
Using 3 mm (size 2.5) needles will give approximately 30 sts x 38 rows to 10 cm (4 in) and add approximately 26 cm (10 in) to the chest size.

ABBREVIATIONS (see also page 140)
3 and 3 rib: K3, p3 all rounds when working in the round (circular or double-pointed needles), alternating (k3, p3 on row 1, p3, k3 on row 2) on two needles.
Moss stitch: K1, p1 all rounds, so the knit stitches are over the purl stitches on the previous round when working in the round (circular or double-pointed needles). Alternate rows of k1, p1 on 2 needles.

Tip: You can knit a pattern – such as the initials of the Guernsey owner – into the gusset. Work this out using graph paper, or embroider it later.

Put the gusset stitches onto stitch holders or waste yarn and continue to work the front and back of the sweater separately using a pair of long needles.

NOTE: For both front and back, it is usual to frame the yoke pattern with a 'strap' of garter stitch, working 5 sts at each side as knit sts so that the patterned area is arranged over the middle 163 (181, 199) sts. You can increase the

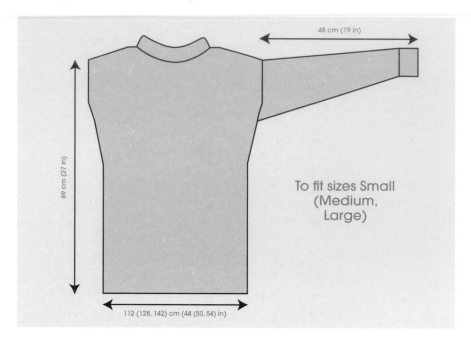

48 cm (19 in)

69 cm (27 in)

To fit sizes Small
(Medium,
Large)

112 (128, 142) cm (44, 50, 54 in)

width of this 'strap' to simplify the design, or to enlarge the sweater.

The front and back are worked in the same way, in your chosen pattern, until armhole measures 20 cm (8 in) deep.

Divide sts: 58 (64, 70) sts for each shoulder, with 57 (62, 68) sts placed on a stitch holder for the neck.

Shape shoulder
Work each shoulder as 12 rows of garter stitch, decreasing one st at the neck edge on 3rd and 7th rows.

Join each pair of shoulders by grafting or knitting off. To do this, put the sts for both shoulders on two needles held parallel and, using a third needle cast off by working into one stitch from each needle for each cast-off stitch.

Neck
Pick up and knit 162 (174, 184) sts around the neck: 57 (63, 68) from each neck stitch holder and 24 from each shoulder edge. Now work k3, p3 rib for 15 rounds, or depth required.

Sleeves
Using 2.25 mm (size 1) circular needle pick up and knit 132 sts around armhole, plus 2 seam sts and 25 gusset sts. (159 sts).

Tip: At this stage, you can add a decorative band or panel (see pattern options below). A band can start at the end of the gusset, but a sleeve panel should start the moment the sleeve is cast on and be worked over the centre sts, with the centre of the pattern marked at the 61st stitch when picking up.

Work the remainder of the gusset by decreasing one st at each end of every 4th row until a single seam stitch remains. Transfer to 4 double-pointed needles when the sleeve becomes too narrow to work easily on the circular needle (or use the magic loop method, see page 141). Once the gusset is complete, continue to work the sleeve in st stitch (with or without a pattern band or panel), maintaining the seam stitch.

Decrease 1 st either side of the seam stitch every 4th round 10

times and then every 5th round until 79 sts remain, knitting last 2 sts together (78 sts). Continue in st stitch until sleeve measures 39 cm (15.5 in) or required length. Finish with 8 cm (3 in) of 3 x 3 rib and cast off firmly in rib.

NOTE: Working the sleeves downwards allows you to try the sweater on and adjust the length as you work.

PATTERNS

These designs are all worked over 173 sts, so the garter stitch band at either side is widened or reduced to take up the additional sts in the larger sizes, leaving the design itself in one size. The charts can be found on pages 107 and 108.

SIMPLE GARTER AND CHEQUER-BOARD

Although this is simple, it will look quite stylish!
Rounds 1-12: purl all sts to match the shoulder band.
Round 13: start the pattern, reducing by 1 st at gussets: k10 (19, 28), work chequer-board pattern over next 153 sts, k10 (19, 28), and repeat for second half of pullover.

Chequer-board stitch
Knitting in the round, over 20 rounds:
Rounds 1 to 10: (k9, p9) repeated 17 times, k9.
Rounds 11 to 20: (p9, k9) repeated 17 times, p9.
Once you have completed the gusset, the pattern will be worked on 2 needles, over 12 rows:
Row 1: (K9, p9) repeated 17 times, k9.
Row 2: (p9, k9) repeated 17 times, p9.
Rows 3 to 10: repeat rows 1 and 2 four times more.
Row 11: as row 2.

Row 12: as row 1.
Rows 13-20: repeat rows 11 and 12 four times more.

NOTE: An alternative to chequer board stitch, with more depth and ridges between the checks, is the Vicar of Morwenstowe slate pattern from Mary Wright's *Cornish Knit Frocks and Guernseys*, which is worked over 28 rounds. You could also consider the Lizard Lattice, over 51 rounds, or Polperro Laughing Boy, over 8 rounds.

Simple variations or additions
- Work a 6st cable either side of your chequer-board. Reduce the garter-stitch edges by 12 sts each side and work as follows:
- **In the round:** rounds 1-5 are k1, p2, k6, p2, k1 before and after the chequer board, then round 6 is k1, p2, C6F, p2, k1 and k1, p2, C6B, p2, k1 respectively at either side (so that the cables are symmetrical).
- **Using 2 needles:** rows 1 and 3 are k1, p2, k6, p2, k1. Row 5 is k1, p2, C6F, p2, k1 and k1, p2, C6B, p2, k1 respectively at either side of the chequer board and rows 2, 4 and 6 are p1, k2, p6, k2, p1.
- Work 2–3 pairs of twisted rib sts either side of your chequer board: reduce the garter edges by 12 sts each side and work T2, p2, T2, p2, T2, p2 each round, or with 2 needles the RS rows will be p2, k2, p2, k2, p2, k2.

Traditional Guernsey pattern
These patterns are all in knit and purl with no cables. Use the charts to help you to follow this. On 2 needles, the even-numbered rounds will have the k and p sts reversed to work in st stitch. Two patterns are given:
- **Chevrons** with moss stitch panels between, worked over 23 sts and 8 rows. This can be done across 161 sts to make 7 chevrons, so you will need to work 6 (15, 24) sts for the garter stitch edges.
- **Moss stitch diamonds** on a st stitch background with garter stitch panels between each, worked over 15 sts and 12 rows. This can be worked across 165 sts to make 11 diamonds. The garter stitch panels will need to be 4 (13, 22) sts wide.
- These patterns may also be used together and worked as horizontal bands. For example, work a garter stitch ridge of 6 rows, followed by a band of diamonds over 12 rows, then 6 more rows of garter stitch, then work the rest of the yoke in chevrons. To keep the garter stitch edges even omit first and last garter sts on the diamond band.
- You will have around 120 rows for the yoke design in total, including the 12 rows of garter stitch at the shoulder and possibly 12 rows as a band from which to launch your pattern. This would therefore be 12 repeats of chevrons or 8 repeats of diamonds.

Other variations
You can also combine these patterns vertically (see photograph on page 104):
- 1 chevron, 3 diamonds, 1 chevron, 3 diamonds, 1 chevron over 159 sts, with garter stitch panels 7 (16, 25) sts wide.
- 2 diamonds, 2 chevrons, 1 diamond, 2 chevrons, 2 diamonds, over 167 sts, with garter stitch edges 3 (12, 21) sts wide.
- Alternate 1 diamond, then 1 chevron, four times, finishing with another diamond, making 167 sts, with garter stitch edges 3 (12, 21) sts wide.
- 3 diamonds, 3 chevrons, then 3 diamonds, making 159 sts, with garter stitch panels 7 (16, 25) sts wide.
- 1 diamond, 5 chevrons,

Chevron pattern

	1	2	3	4	5	6	7	8	9	10	11	12	13	14	15	16	17	18	19	20	21	22	23
8						x															x		
7		x	x			x												x			x	x	
6								x									x						
5	x						x								x								x
4									x					x									
3		x	x							x			x							x	x		
2											x		x										
1	x				x							x							x				x

KEY

⊠ p on RS; k on WS   ☐ k on RS; p on WS

Stiches for chevron pattern
Round 1   P1, k2, p1, k7, p1, k7, p1, k2, p1.
Round 2   K10, p1, k1, p1, k10
Round 3   K1, p2, k6, p1, k3, p1, k6, p2, k1.
Round 4   K8, p1, k5, p1, k8.
Round 5   P1, k6, p1, k7, p1, k6, p1.
Round 6   K6, p1, k9, p1, k6.
Round 7   K1, p2, k2, p1, k11, p1, k2, p2, k1.
Round 8   K4, p1, k13, p1, k4.

Chevron pattern with repeats

KEY
☒ p on RS; k on WS ☐ k on RS; p on WS

Moss diamond pattern

Row	1	2	3	4	5	6	7	8	9	10	11	12	13	14	15
12								x							
11	x						x		x						x
10						x	x	x							
9	x				x		x		x		x				x
8				x		x		x		x		x			
7	x		x		x		x		x		x		x		x
6				x		x		x		x		x			
5	x				x		x		x		x				x
4						x		x		x					
3	x						x		x						x
2								x							
1	x														x

KEY
☒ p on RS; k on WS ☐ k on RS; p on WS

Stiches for moss diamond pattern

Round 1 P1, k13, p1.
Round 2 K7, p1, k7.
Round 3 P1, k5, p1, k1, p1, k5, p1.
Round 4 K5, p1, k1, p1, k1, p1, k5.
Round 5 P1, k3, p1, k1, p1, k1, p1, k1, p1, k3, p1.
Round 6 K3, p1, k1, p1, k1, p1, k1, p1, k1, p1, k3.K2, p2, k2, P3,
Round 7 k1, p1, k1, p1, k1, p1, k1, p1, k1, p1, k1, p1, k1, p1.
Round 8 K3, p1, k1, p1, k1, p1, k1, p1, k1, p1, k3.
Round 9 P1, k3, p1, k1, p1, k1, p1, k1, p1, k3, p1.
Round 10 K5, p1, k1, k1, k1, p1, k5.
Round 11 P1, k5, p1, k1, p1, k5, p1.
Round 12 K7, p1, k7.

1 diamond, making 145 sts, with garter stitch panels of 14 (23, 32) sts or make a stronger vertical line each side of the diamonds. These are all symmetrical, and add to an odd number of sts, allowing the garter stitch edges to be the same on both sides.

Adding patterns to the sleeves
When knitting down the sleeves, you may wish to work a band of diamonds, bordered with garter stitch, or a simple garter stitch border, or the chequerboard pattern. Normally a sleeve pattern will stop at the end of the gusset, so you have around 40-50 rows to play with while tapering the gusset.

On a traditional fisherman's sweater, the rest of the sleeve would be plain. As an alternative, work a central vertical line of diamonds to the cuff. Or, if you have used cables on the yoke, try a cable with a narrow reverse stitch border.

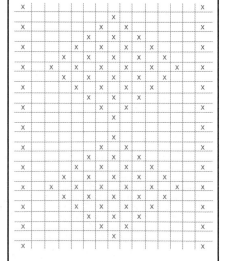

Moss pattern with repeats

KEY
☒ p on RS; k on WS
☐ k on RS; p on WS

Ryeland fleece

The Ryeland is a 'typical' sheep. Being small and gentle (and short legs make it harder to leap over fences), they are a favourite among smallholders and are also sought after for their meat. As they have a tendency to put on weight if fed concentrates or on rich pastures, they are also good for sparse pastures and a total grass diet and consequently work well under organic husbandry.

The Ryeland has been famous since the Middle Ages for its fine wool. The abundant fleece is well-suited for making clothes. It is said Queen Elizabeth I was so fond of her 'Lemster' wool stockings that she insisted on all her wool stockings being from Ryeland wool (although she quickly developed a taste for silk stockings!).

The sheep are a small, short-woolled version of the white, fat-tailed sheep so are no doubt distantly related to Roman imports and Romneys rather than to northern short-tailed sheep. The ewes weigh 50–60 kg (110–132 lbs) and rams 75–80 kg (165–176 lbs).

A breed society was formed in 1903 to try to ensure the survival of these sheep, which were not competing well with the more commercial Leicester-based breeds.

Having the help of a breed society did not ensure success for the Ryeland sheep, and by the 1970s it was again facing a decline. In 1973, with less than 500 registered breeding ewes The Rare Breeds Survival Trust found Ryeland sheep to be Endangered, however, today with 3,000 registered breeding ewes they are now classified as a Native Breed. This success is partly due to the popularity of the Ryeland in small flocks, and also the attractions of its white and coloured wool and encouragement of the development of the Coloured Ryeland, which has no white genes and so will consistently breed coloured progeny.

BREED AT A GLANCE

Sheep type: Native.

Appearance: Ryelands are small, with dense, short, white fleece, a slightly compact and tubby appearance, no horns, short woolly legs, dark feet, and something of the teddy bear in general style. Ryelands can also come in a coloured version, which is a lovely brown-grey.

Rare breeds status: None.

Further information:

UK breed society: www.ryelandfbs.com.

History: The Ryeland is said to have been specifically developed in the 12th century by the monks at Leominster near Hereford, on the borderlands between England and Wales, to make fine wool for cloth. They were also used to graze land where rye was being grown, to stimulate the growth, hence the name.

carded fleece

mid 4-ply yarn

dark Aran yarn

scoured fleece

light Aran yarn

pale DK yarn

mid DK yarn

FLEECE FACT FILE
Fleece weight: 2–2.75 kg (4–5 lbs)
Staple length: 7.5–10 cm (3–4 in)
Micron count: 28–32
Crimp: Fine
Handle: Soft
Natural colours: White, black, grey, brown
Mixed colours: Greys and browns
Lustre: High

dark DK yarn

dark 4-ply yarn

Close-up of knitted DK sample

raw fleece

Ryeland yarn

Ryeland is typical downland wool, being short, resilient, stretchy, and with good insulating properties. It has little kemp, though this may be coloured in the white sheep, and the crimp is indistinct. Do not, however, try felting it as you could spend a long time not getting a result!

White and Coloured Ryeland wools are very similar and can be spun alone or mixed to create an intermediate shade of yarn. The Coloured wool, which is mainly grey but with brown highlights, is particularly attractive and makes a beautiful heathered yarn. The white wool is one of the creamiest in colour of all the white wools, being similar to that of Blue-faced Leicester sheep. It is often woven to make good tweeds and rugs.

Despite its reputation with Queen Elizabeth I and her fine stockings, Ryeland's bouncy downland wool means that nowadays it is better suited to woollen spun thicker yarns, Double Knitting and above, and works well for outer garments. Because it does not felt

easily, it will also retain the stitch definition in cabled and textured garments over years of wear. Selection for finer wool in small flocks will reduce the micron count and make for softer yarns.

We have chosen Ryeland for a child's jacket. This is worked in two strands, so it is possible to consider using one each of white, mid-coloured, or coloured Ryeland yarn to make a paler or darker tweedy version. Ryeland yarn will also work for the patterns we have provided for Black Welsh Mountain, Galway, Hebridean, Jacob, Manx Loagthan or Zwartbles yarns.

Soft and airy, Ryeland yarn is also resilient, making it perfect for textured stitches and cable designs that will retain their shape after wear and washing.

Ryeland child's hooded jacket

by Myra Mortlock
and Sue Blacker

This textured jacket is perfect to wear outdoors on a chilly autumn day. It is knitted using two strands of Ryeland yarn in stocking stitch, while seeds of purl stitches add visual interest. The seed stitches are continued on to the edges of the garment and are a simple way to add texture to the fabric.

You can use one colour of yarn, or choose one strand of white and one of coloured for a tweedy effect.

The loop fastening means there is no need to knit buttonholes, and you can use buttons or toggles. Finish the hood with a tassel, or replace it with a small collar.

YARN REQUIREMENTS

Ryeland worsted-weight/DK

• Total amount of wool by weight and approximate length
Small: 500 g/1,110 m (1,190 yds)
Large: 700 g/1,540 m (1,666 yds)
• Yarn used doubled throughout. Use a single colour throughout, or equal amounts of two different colours for a tweedy effect.

Method

NOTE: working with two strands of yarn is easy, but occasionally you will only pick up one, so check each row. You will usually find the mistake on the next row. Use a crochet hook to pick up and link in the extra strand.

BACK (make 1)

Using 5.5 mm (size 9) needles and 2 strands of yarn together, cast on 50 (60) sts.
Welt pattern:
Row 1: K1, p1, repeat to end.
Row 2: P1 (wool back, slip 1 knitwise, wool forward p1), repeat to last st, k1.
Row 3: as row 1.
Row 4: as row 2, but for larger size increase by 1 st at each end of row 50 (62) sts.
Begin main pattern.

Main pattern
Row 1: Knit.
Row 2: Purl.
Row 3: K3 *p1, k3*, repeat from * to* to last 3 sts, p1, k2.
Row 4: Purl.
Row 5: Knit.
Row 6: Purl.
Row 7: K5 *p1, k3*, repeat from * to* to last st, k1.
Row 8: Purl.
Repeat rows 1-8 until work measures 24 (26) cm (9.5 (11.5) in).

Shape raglan

Right side facing, continue to knit pattern while decreasing sts as follows:
Row 1: cast off 2 sts, work to end.
Row 2: cast off 2 sts, purl to end.
Row 3: K2 tog, work in pattern to last 2 sts, k2 tog.
Row 4: Purl.
Repeat rows 3 and 4 until 37 (44) sts remain.
Decrease at each end of every row until 15 (18) sts remain.
Cast off.

FRONTS (make 2)

Using 5.5 mm (size 9) needles and 2 strands of yarn together, cast on 26 (32) sts.
Work 4 rows of welt as given for back.
Work seed stitch band of 5 sts at centre edge of both fronts (first row k1, p1, second row p1, k1), continuing in main pattern for rest of row until work measures 24 (26) cm (9.5 (11.5) in).

Shape raglan

At side edge cast off 5 (6) sts.
Work one row without shaping.
Decrease one st at side edge on next and following alternate rows to 19 (23) sts.

Shape neck

At neck edge, cast off 5 (6) sts.
Decrease 1 st at both ends of

every alternate row until 4 sts remain.
Next row: K2 tog twice.
Next row: K2 tog and cast off last st.
Repeat to make second side, reversing shaping.

SLEEVES (make 2)

Using 5.5 mm (size 9) needles and 2 strands of yarn together, cast on 26 (31) sts.
Work welt as for back.
Change to pattern and work first 4 rows.
Row 5: K1, increase in the next st, work in pattern to the last 2 sts, increase in next st, k1.
Row 6: purl.
Row 7: Work pattern row.
Row 8: purl.
Row 9: increase at both ends as row 5.
Row 10: purl.
Repeat rows 7-10 until work measures 24 (26) cm (9.5 (11.5) in) and you have a total of 46 (55) sts.

Shape raglan

Maintaining pattern, decrease as follows:
Row 1: right side facing, cast off 2 sts, work to end.
Row 2: cast off 2 sts, work to end.
Decrease at each end of every row to 12 (14) sts, then alternate rows to 10 (12) sts.
Cast off.

HOOD (make 1)

The hood is worked as one piece, and follows the main pattern with a band of seed st along the edge. You start knitting at one corner of the neck and work up and over the head, with a centre-back seam.

Using 5.5 mm (size 9) needles and 2 strands of yarn together, cast on 6 (8) sts.
Row 1: (K1, p1) repeat to end.

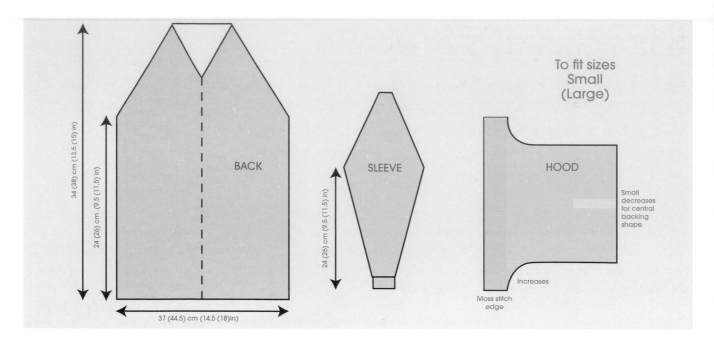

BACK

34 (38) cm (13.5 (15) in)

24 (26) cm (9.5 (11.5) in)

37 (44.5) cm (14.5 (18)in)

SLEEVE

24 (26) cm (9.5 (11.5) in)

HOOD

Small decreases for central backing shape

Increases

Moss stitch edge

Row 2: K1, k twice into next st. (p1, k1) to end.
Row 3: K1, p1, k1, p1, k1, purl to end of row.
Row 4: (Knit row) continue, increasing one st at start of this and alternate rows to 14 (17) sts, introducing main 8-row pattern and maintaining 6 st seed stitch edging.

Back/side neck edge

Cast on another 18 (22) sts.
Work 6 rows in pattern.
At centre-back edge, increase 1 st at start of next row.
Work 5 rows, until work measures approximately 8 (10) cm (3 (4) in) from neck edge cast on.
At centre back, increase 1 st at start of next row.
Continue in pattern to 43 (52) cm (17 (20) in) from 18 (22) st cast on.
Next row: at centre-back edge k1, k2 tog. Work to end of row.
Work 5 rows, then repeat decrease.
Work 6 rows.
Next row: at centre-back edge cast off 18 (22) sts.
Work one row.
Decrease on alternate rows to match other side of hood.
Cast off last 6 (8) sts.

MAKE UP

For general advice on making up garments see page 141.
With wrong sides facing, pin or tack shoulders together and then sew. Fit sleeves to armholes and then sew side and sleeve seams.
Fold hood in half, pin centre join on wrong side and sew. Pin centre back of hood to centre back of body. Pin or tack lower hood edge to body and sew. If liked, fold hood edge inwards and sew down lightly.
Sew toggles on appropriate side for boy or girl.
Make five lengths of I-cord – a knitted tube – for the loops and attach to meet toggles.
To make an I-cord, using two 5.5 mm (size 9) double-pointed needles, cast on 3 sts and k one row. Move the stitches to the opposite end of the needle and knit again, pulling the yarn across the back of the work to close the tube. Repeat until required length. Cast off.
To make a tassel for the hood, cut a piece of card 16 cm (6.5 in) wide. Take two strands of yarn and wind them around the card ten times. Do not cut yarn. Tie start end of yarn to working end. Turn card over and cut

threads opposite the tie. Bind yarn around threads to make tassel. Sew through tassel and secure. Attach tassel to hood.

ADJUSTING THE SIZE OF THE JACKET

You can make the jacket longer in the body or sleeves, but you will need more yarn.
• **To make the jacket larger overall,** knit on one size larger needles, but note that this will result in a looser and less wind-proof version.
• **To make the jacket wider,** you will need to adjust the raglan sleeve and neck edge. To do this, add stitches in groups of 6, allowing 2 for the first part of the decreases (2 extra rows), 2 for the second part (one extra row) and leaving 2 extra at the end, which creates 3 extra rows in length. This will give around 5 cm (2 in) per 6 stitches. If adding more, increase the number decreased in the first two rows of the raglan shaping. You can also add stitches all the way up, to increase the size of the neck. An easier way to enlarge the front is to make the seed stitch bands 6 stitches wider.

Shetland fleece

Shetland sheep have evolved to survive the harsh environment of the islands where they have traditionally been farmed. Shetland wool is either from the breed, from sheep farmed on the Shetland Islands, or sometimes from both! Today organic pedigree Shetland sheep on the Islands have European Union denomination of origin status.

Shetland fleece is a non-lustre, fine, soft and silky wool with a distinctly tiny, dense crimp. Some fleeces can be matted if shorn late, and the sheep can begin to shed them unless shorn on time.

Its Viking heritage can been found in the Norsk nomenclature for fleece colours and markings. The best-known names of the colours are the moorit brown and katmogit or gulmogit (Mouflon markings) greys. There are 11 main colours and 35 markings, but in 1996 a Shetland Sheep Society survey found sufficient variations to provide a poster of 63 of these markings.

Adult sheep weigh in at 35–40 kg (77–88 lbs) for ewes and 45–55 kg (99–121 lbs) for rams on the mainland, but as little as 22 kg (48.4 lbs) for a ewe on the Islands.

The Shetland Flockbook society was established in 1927 in Shetland to protect the purity of the breed. The Shetland Sheep Society was set up for the same purpose on the mainland in 1985.

Some Shetland sheep work on conservation grazing in the UK. The breed has been imported into North America.

The Rare Breeds Survival Trust classified Shetland sheep as Endangered in 1977, but by 2008 there were over 800 registered ewes and nearly 300 rams. Today, breeders are focusing on ensuring that the variety of markings is preserved.

BREED AT A GLANCE

Sheep type: Primitive.

Appearance: One of Britain's smallest sheep. The rams usually have curling horns, but the ewes usually do not. They come in a wide variety of colours, which have been the basis of the Fair Isle knitting. Each colour and marking pattern has its own Norse name.

Rare breeds status: Native in UK. Recovering in US.

Further information: UK breed society: www.shetland-sheep.org.uk. Shetland Flock Book breed society: www.shetland-sheep.co.uk. North American breed society: www.shetland-sheep.org.

History: A hardy, self sufficient northern short-tailed sheep with Viking ancestry dating back to the 8th century on the Shetland Islands off the coast of Scotland. They have mainly been farmed on the highlands and islands, or on parklands for their attractive appearance.

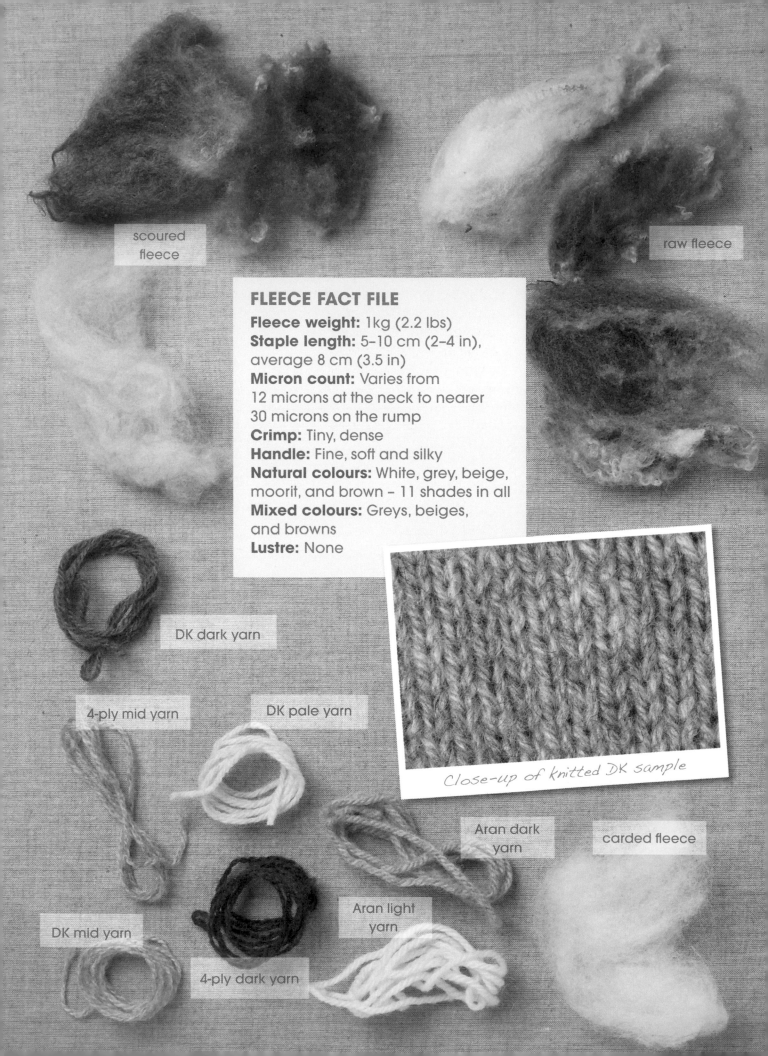

scoured
fleece

raw fleece

FLEECE FACT FILE
Fleece weight: 1kg (2.2 lbs)
Staple length: 5–10 cm (2–4 in),
average 8 cm (3.5 in)
Micron count: Varies from
12 microns at the neck to nearer
30 microns on the rump
Crimp: Tiny, dense
Handle: Fine, soft and silky
Natural colours: White, grey, beige,
moorit, and brown – 11 shades in all
Mixed colours: Greys, beiges,
and browns
Lustre: None

DK dark yarn

4-ply mid yarn

DK pale yarn

Close-up of knitted DK sample

Aran dark
yarn

carded fleece

DK mid yarn

Aran light
yarn

4-ply dark yarn

Shetland yarn

Like the colours and markings, Shetland fleeces can vary considerably between different animals and within a single fleece. This diversity makes them very interesting for hand-spinning. It is also possible to achieve both a lace-weight yarn and a thicker yarn from the same fleece.

Shetland sheep may once have had a double coat like the North Ronaldsay but now have a single coat of very fine fleece, although it can vary significantly from only 12 microns at the neck to nearer 30 microns on the rump.

The fine wool from Shetland sheep was originally used mainly to knit stockings, exported to the UK and the Netherlands from the 17th century onwards. Shetland lace-work shawls – including the famous ring shawls that are so fine they will pass through a wedding ring – were also an export until the early 20th century, when Fair Isle pullovers, hats and mittens began to take over.

The wool is versatile, ideal for lace-weight or chunky yarns, soft fabrics or more solid tweeds, and of course you have generally at least five and possibly up to 11 natural colours. The wool does also dye and felt quite well, so it is better for colour work than for textured knitting.

We have chosen a fine scarf and a patterned waistcoat to illustrate the versatility of Shetland wool.

You could also use Shetland yarns for non-lustre versions of the Blue-faced Leicester blanket or the Gotland beret patterns, the Manx Loagthan accessories, or the North Ronaldsay or Ryeland designs.

Shetland yarns were used for the original, colourful Fair Isles designs, but the natural shades offer plenty of variety to the knitter. The yarn – from laceweight to Aran – is sturdy but of varying softness so not all will be suitable for childrens' clothes.

YARN USER'S GUIDE
Good for ...
- Hand-spinning
- Variety of yarn thicknesses and natural colours
- Dyeing
- Felting

Not so good for ...
- Textured stitches
- Worsted yarns

Shetland spot waistcoat

by Sasha Kagan

This classic retro style was originally designed by Sasha in the 1970s, but is just as easy to wear now! The original pattern has been updated and adapted for Blacker Yarns 4-ply yarns. Relaxed and casual or stylish, you can dress it up or down happily. The four pockets are a nice feature but all of them or just the upper ones can be omitted if you wish. The back is worked in a neat stretchy twisted rib to fit snugly, so you can wear it as part of a suit as well. The fronts are worked in the Fair Isle design and all the borders are added afterwards, as are the pocket borders and linings.

DESIGNER PROFILE

Sasha Kagan is a name synonymous with the renaissance in contemporary British knitwear. She has been designing and making knitwear since the 1960s and is renowned for her lively use of colour and distinctive patterns.

YARN REQUIREMENTS

Pure Shetland wool 4-ply yarn
• Total amount of wool by weight and approximate length:
200 (250, 250, 300, 300) g/700 (875, 875, 1,050, 1,050) m (760 (950, 950, 1,140, 1,140) yds) Shetland Dark (A)
50 g/175 m (190 yds) Shetland Moorit
50 g/175 m (190 yds) Shetland Fawn
50 g/175 m (190 yds) Classic Turquoise
50 g/175 m (190 yds) Classic Purple

MEASUREMENTS
Around the bust: 86 (91, 96, 101, 106) cm (34 (36, 38, 40, 42) in)
Garment bust measurement: 91 cm (96, 101, 106, 111) cm (36 (38, 40, 42, 44) in)
Length: 58 (58, 58, 61, 61) cm (23 (23, 23, 24, 24) in)
Instructions are given for the smallest size first, followed by larger sizes brackets

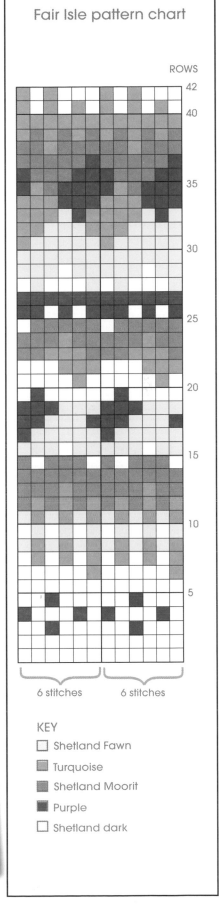

Fair Isle pattern chart

SKILL LEVEL

NEEDLES & NOTIONS
One pair each 2.25 mm (size 1), 2.75 mm (size 2), 3 mm (size 3) needles
Five 2 cm (¾ in) buttons

TENSION
Approx 27 sts x 29 rows = 10 cm (4 in) over chart pattern on 3 mm (size 3) needles
Approx 32 sts x 26 rows = 10 cm (4 in) over twisted rib pattern on 2.25 mm (size 1) needles
Adjust needle size to give required tension.

ABBREVIATIONS (see also page 140)
Twisted rib: Row 1 (RS): *k1-b, p1* repeat to end. Row 2: k1, P1-b* repeat to end.

ROWS

6 stitches   6 stitches

KEY
☐ Shetland Fawn
▨ Turquoise
▨ Shetland Moorit
■ Purple
☐ Shetland dark

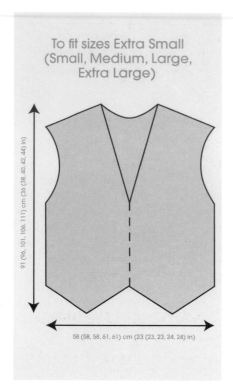

To fit sizes Extra Small (Small, Medium, Large, Extra Large)

91 (96, 101, 106, 111) cm (36 (38, 40, 42, 44) in)

58 (58, 58, 61, 61) cm (23 (23, 23, 24, 24) in)

Method

BACK (work one)

Using 2.25 mm (size 1) needles and A cast on 122 (130, 140, 150, 158) sts. Work in twisted rib, at the same time increase 1 st at both ends of 8th row, then every following 6th row until there are 144 (152, 162, 172, 180) sts, keeping rib correct.
Continue without shaping until work measures 23 (23, 23, 24, 24) cm (9 (9, 9, 9.5, 9.5) in) from cast on edge.

Shape armholes

Cast off 9 (10, 10, 11, 11) sts at beginning of next 2 rows. Then decrease 1 st at both ends of next and every alt row until 110 (112, 116, 118, 120) sts remain. Continue without further shaping until work measures 45 (45, 45, 47, 47.5) cm (17.75 (17.75, 17.75, 18.75, 18.75) in).

Shape shoulders

Cast off 12 sts at beginning of next 6 rows. Cast off remaining 38 (38, 42, 44, 46) sts.

RIGHT FRONT
(work one)

Using 3 mm (size 3) needles and A cast on 2 sts. Refer to chart and repeat the 42 rows to end. Start chart on sts 1 and 2, adding more of chart at start and end of rows as sts increase.

Extra Small

Row 1: K twice into first st, K1.
Row 2: P3.
Row 3: Knit, increasing 1 st in first st and last st (5 sts).
Repeat rows 3 and 4 five times.
Row 15: K, increasing 1 st in first st and last st (35 sts).
Row 16: Cast on 2 sts, p to end.
Row 17-28: Repeat rows 15 and 16 six times (61 sts).
Row 29: K across row.
Row 30: Cast on 2 sts, p to end (63 sts).

Small

Work rows 1 to 3 as for Extra Small.
Row 4: Cast on 3 sts, p to last 2 sts, increase in next st, p1 (9 sts).
Rows 5-10: repeat rows 3 and 4 three times (27 sts).
Row 11: K, increasing 1 st in first st and last st.
Row 12: cast on 2 sts, p to end.
Rows 13-30: repeat rows 11 and 12 nine times (67 sts).

Medium

Work rows 1 to 4 as for Small.
Rows 5-14: repeat rows 3 and 4 five times (39 sts).
Row 15: K, increase 1 st in first st and last st.
Row 16: cast on 2 sts, p to end.
Rows 17-30: repeat rows 15 and 16 seven times (71 sts).

Large

Work rows 1 to 4 as for Small.
Rows 5-16: repeats rows 3 and 4 six times (45 sts).
Row 17: K, increasing 1 st in first st and last st.
Row 18: cast on 2 sts, p to end.
Rows 19-30: repeat rows 17 and 18 six times (73 sts).

Extra Large

Work rows 1 to 4 as for Small.
Rows 5-20: repeat rows 3 and 4 eight times (57 sts).
Row 21: K, increasing 1 st in first st and last st.
Row 22: cast on 2 sts, p to end.
Rows 23-30: repeat rows 21 and 22 four times (77 sts)

All sizes

Work in pattern for 7.5 cm (3 in) ending with a WS row.

Work lower pocket

Next Row: K18 (20, 22, 23, 25) sts, cast off 27 sts, k to end.
Next row: P18 (20, 22, 23, 25) sts, cast on 27 sts, p to end.
Continue in pattern, increasing 1 st at end of first row (RS) and 22nd row after pocket rows. 65 (69, 73, 75, 79) sts.
Continue until straight edge at centre front measures 17.5 (17.75, 17.75, 20.5, 20.5) cm (7 (7, 7, 8, 8) in) ending on WS row.

Shape front neck edge

Decrease 1 st at neck on next and every 5th row 14 (14, 15, 16, 17) times. Continue until work measures 20.5 (20.5, 20.5, 21.5, 21.5) cm (8 (8, 8, 8.5, 8.5) in) at side edge, ending on RS row.

Shape armholes

Cast off 6 (7, 7, 8, 8) sts, p to end. Work 1 row then dec 1 st at beginning of next and every following alternate row 19 (21, 24, 24, 27) times.
When work measures 21.5 (21.5, 21.5, 23, 23) cm (8.5 (8.5, 8.5, 9, 9) in) along side edge, ending with WS row, work Upper Pocket as for Lower Pocket, directly above Lower Pocket.

Continue in pattern until work measures 42.5 (42.5, 42.5, 45, 45) cm (16.75 (16.75, 16.75, 17.75, 17.75) in) ending with RS row.

Shape shoulder

Cast off 8 (9, 9, 9, 9) sts at start of next row. Work 1 row.

Cast off 9 sts at start of next and following alternate row.

LEFT FRONT
(work one)

Using 3 mm (size 3) needles and A cast on 2 sts. Refer to chart and repeat the 42 rows to end. Start chart on sts 1 and 2, adding more of chart at beginning and end as you increase. Work shaping at bottom as follows:

Extra Small
Row 1: K twice into first st, k1.
Row 2: P3.
Row 3: K, increasing 1 st in first st and last st (5 sts).
Row 4: P1, inc in next st, p to end, cast on 2 sts (8 sts).
Row 5-14: Repeat rows 3 and 4 five times (33 sts).
Row 15: K, increasing 1 st in first st and last st.
Row 16: P to end, cast on 2 sts.
Row 17-28: Repeat rows 15 and 16 six times (61 sts).
Row 29: K across row.
Row 30: P to end, cast on 2 sts (63 sts).

Small
Work rows 1 to 3 as for Extra Small.
Row 4: P1, increase in next st, p to end, cast on 3 sts (9 sts).
Rows 5-10: repeat rows 3 and 4 three times (27 sts).
Row 11: K, increasing 1 st in first st and last st.
Row 12: P to end, cast on 2 sts.
Rows 13-30: repeat rows 11 and 12 nine times (67 sts).

Medium
Work rows 1 to 4 as for Small.
Rows 5-14: repeat rows 3 and 4 five times (39 sts).
Row 15: K, increase 1 st in first st and last st.
Row 16: P to end, cast on 2 sts.
Rows 17-30: repeat rows 15 and 16 seven times (71 sts).

Large
Work rows 1 to 4 as for Small.

Rows 5-16: repeats rows 3 and 4 six times (45 sts).
Row 17: K, increasing 1 st in first st and last st.
Row 18: P to end, cast on 2 sts.
Rows 19-30: repeat rows 17 and 18 six times (73 sts).

Extra Large
Work rows 1 to 4 as for Small.
Rows 5-20: repeat rows 3 and 4 eight times (57 sts).
Row 21: K, increasing 1 st in first st and last st.
Row 22: P to end, cast on 2 sts.
Rows 23-30: repeat rows 21 and 22 four times (77 sts).

Complete as for right front, reversing shaping and pocket placements.

FINISHING

Darn loose ends into own colours. Block all pieces and press lightly on WS avoiding ribbing. Join shoulder seams.

FRONT BORDERS
(make one)

Borders start at point at bottom of left front and extend to point at bottom of right front. Measure as you work - it should fit snugly when stretched slightly.

Using 2.25 mm (size 1) needles and A cast on 2 sts.
Work k1, p1 twisted rib casting on 2 sts at beginning of every alternate row until 12 sts. Continue until start of straight front edge on right front.
Next row: Rib 4 cast off 3 sts for buttonhole, rib 5.
Next row: Rib 5, cast on 3 sts, rib 4.
Mark 4 more buttonholes on right front - one at point where neckline shaping starts 3 evenly between. Continue in rib, making buttonholes and until border fits up right side of neck around and down other side, ending at corner of peak.

Starting at edge where shaping at beginning finished, cast off 2 sts at beginning of next and every alt row until 2 sts remain. Cast off.

LOWER-EDGE BORDER
(make 2)

Using 2.25 mm (size 1) needles and A cast on 2 sts.
Work in k1 p1 twisted rib casting on 2 sts at beginning of every alt row until there are 12 sts. Continue in rib until border fits from front point to side seam. Cast off.

ARMHOLE BORDERS
(work two)

Using 2.25 mm (size 1) needles, with RS facing and A, pick up and k 1 st for each row on front armhole up to shoulder, then the same number of sts down back armhole. Work 6 rows in k1 p1 twisted rib. Cast off in rib.

POCKET BORDERS
(work four)

Using 2.25 mm (size 1) needles, with RS facing and A, pick up and k 26 sts from bottom edges of pocket slits. Work 6 rows in k1, p1 twisted rib. Cast off in rib.

POCKET LININGS
(work four)

Using 2.75 mm (size 2) needles, with RS facing and A, pick up and K sts across top of pocket slits. Work 2.5 in (6 cm) in st st. Cast off.

MAKING UP

Sew down the edges of pocket borders and linings. Join lower edge borders to front borders and points. Sew front borders. Join side seams, making sure the lower edge of the border is sewn to the back at the base. Attach buttons.

Shetland feather and fan scarf

by Rita Taylor

This scarf is worked in an easy but very attractive lace design called Feather and Fan, which is deservedly one of the most popular lace patterns. It only uses one row of pattern plus three further rows all in knit stitch for a four-row repeat, so it is excellent for beginners. In softest Double Knitting Shetland yarn, the scarf is quick to make and goes back to Shetland lace roots with a modern update of a ribbed middle section to fit cosily with less bulk around the neck. It is worked in two pieces and grafted together to make the ends match perfectly.

Method

First section
Using 5 mm (size 8) needles cast on 55 sts and knit 2 rows.

Begin pattern
Row 1: *K1, (k2tog) 3 times, (yf, k1) 5 times, yf, (k2tog) 3 times; rep from * to last st, k1.
Row 2: Knit.
Row 3: Knit.
Row 4: Knit.
Continue working these 4 rows until work measures 30 cm (12 in) ending with a 4th row. Increase 1 at each end of last row and leave 57 sts on a holder.

Second section
Work as for first section, but

YARN REQUIREMENTS
Shetland worsted weight yarn
• Total amount of wool by weight and approximate length:
200 g/440 m (476 yds)

instead of leaving sts on holder, continue in k3, p3 rib until work measures 173 cm (68 in). Knit one row.

Join the two sections
Graft or cast off together the

SKILL LEVEL

FINISHED SIZES
80 in (203 cm) long

NEEDLES & NOTIONS
One pair 5 mm (size 8) knitting needles

TENSION
There is no set gauge for this pattern.

second section with the sts from the holder from the first section to complete.

Zwartbles fleece

Zwartbles – the name means black with a white blaze – were initially bred to produce milk and meat, and their thick coats were ideal to protect them from the cold, wet and windy weather. The dense fleece is generally considered as suitable only for making carpets, but enlightened spinners and knitters are starting to use it to create hard-wearing garments.

The fleece of the Zwartbles has virtually no kemp, but it does become slightly tinged with grey when older. The sun bleaches the wool to a reddish brown, so the sheep can appear red in the fields. Because it is so thick, the fleece makes a resilient yarn.

As well as the blaze Zwartbles sheep should have two white socks on the back feet, sometimes also the front feet, and a white tip to the long tail (which is never docked). With their black-and-white markings they are similar to the Balwen Welsh mountain sheep, but the fleece is very different, being denser, consistent, finer and darker. Any white or silvery fibres are considered undesirable by breeders.

The sheep have bare legs; black, striped or white feet; large, dark Leicester-style ears; and no horns. They weigh in at 85 kg (187 lbs) for adult ewes and 100 kg (220 lbs) for rams.

In the Netherlands, the breed was recorded as rare by the Dutch Rare Breeds Survival Trust in the 1970s. Recently the easily managed, easy-lambing Zwartbles has seen a revival. In the Netherlands they are still used as milk sheep, particularly for cheese, and work as a complementary enterprise with dairy cattle.

Zwartbles is increasingly popular in the UK, where it was first farmed in the 1990s, as a commercial meat sheep. There are now more than 5,000 Zwartbles in over 200 registered flocks. However, the finer, younger fleeces are not yet seen as worth using for knitting yarns. This is a shame as some of the dark wool is really lovely, and it has a nice resilience.

While a minority in the UK, and not common in the Netherlands, the Zwartbles is no longer rare. No flocks are listed in North America.

BREED AT A GLANCE

Sheep type: European.
Appearance: Black with a white blaze on the nose; no horns.
Rare breeds status: None.
Further information: UK breed society: www.zwartbles.org.
History: Developed in the 19th century in Friesland in the Netherlands, when the native Fresian and Drenthe breeds were crossed to create a sheep that would clean-up land that had been grazed by dairy herds.

5-ply Guernsey
worsted yarn

DK yarn

FLEECE FACT FILE

Fleece weight: 2–3 kg (4–6.5 lbs)
Staple length: 10–12.5 cm (4–5 in)
Micron count: 31–34
Crimp: Indistinct
Handle: Crisp
Natural colours: Predominantly
black, with some brown
Mixed colours: None
Lustre: None

Aran yarn

olive-dyed
Zwartbles/mohair
DK yarn

Close-up of Aran knitted sample

carded fleece

scoured
fleece

raw fleece

Zwartbles yarn

Zwartbles sheep are still relatively new to the knitting wool industry, and yarns made from their fleece are not yet widely used. It is worth some attention as this dark wool has a different texture from dark-coloured yarns made from Black Welsh Mountain and Hebridean wool.

Zwartbles fleece that has been bleached red by the sun will come out as a rich bitter chocolate colour when spun. A fleece that has been trimmed of any red wool will be a true black.

As with most larger downland sheep, it is well worth getting shearling wool for the best quality. Some Zwartbles wool is very soft and fine, but the average is more like a dark Jacob. We have found that Zwartbles blends beautifully with mohair to create an attractive anthracite silvered black yarn, with the mohair emphasising the dark of the Zwartbles and taking away the off-black colour. This dyes well with olive or purple to make attractive dark yarns.

Dark, crisp and durable, Zwartbles yarn gives great stitch definition and is best used for outer garments.

The yarn produces dark rugs and tweeds and does not felt easily. The crimp is indistinct and woolly but the yarn is versatile, spinning from 4-ply to Aran. It is more crisp than soft in finish.

We have chosen a cardigan with a textured cable design for our Zwartbles yarn, as it is an ideal wool for outer garments and will last well, maintaining the pattern after wash and wear. Other designs suitable for Zwartbles yarn include the Black Welsh Mountain waistcoat, Galway Aran sweater, Hebridean bag and cushion, Herdwick accessories, North Ronaldsay waistcoat and Ryeland child's jacket.

Climbing vine cardigan

By Sian Brown

This attractive cardigan has the climbing vine cable, bordered with a neat twisted cable, on either side of the front, mirrored on the back and on each sleeve, all set on a reverse stocking stitch background.

Changing the needle size on the body enables the garment to fit without needing to increase or decrease the number of stitches or adjust the design. The cardigan has a deep welt and wide front bands rising into a wrap collar. It is finished with a single feature button or can be left open as a short stylish jacket.

DESIGNER PROFILE

Sian Brown uses natural wool for most of her designs and loves its tactile feel. She spent the first years of her career designing machine knits for retail suppliers and now designs handknits for magazines, yarn companies and book publishers.

YARN REQUIREMENTS

Pure Zwartbles Worsted weight/DK yarn
UK size 12: 450 g/990 m (1,071 yds)
UK size 14: 500 g/1,100 m (1,190 yds)
UK size 16: 550 g/1,210 m (1,309 yds)
UK size 18: 600 g/1,320 m (1,428 yds)
UK size 20: 650 g/1,430 m (1,547 yds)
UK size 22: 700 g/1,540 m (1,666 yds)

If you wish you can substitute Zwartbles blended with 50% mohair for a softer handle and slight sheen, which enables the cables to be seen even though it is a little more fluffy.

Method

Climbing vine and cable panel (worked over 26 sts)
1st row: (WS) P3, k3, p3, k3, p4, C2BP, k5, p3.
2nd row: Sl 1 pw, k2, p4, C2F, k1, T2B, k2, p3, T2F, k1, p3, k2, sl 1pw.
3rd row: Sl 1pw, p2, k3, p2, k4, p2, k1, p3, C2BP, k3, p2, sl 1pw.
4th row: C3L, p3, k3, T2B, p1, k1, C2B, p3, T2F, p3, C3R.
5th row: P3, k7, C2Fp, p2, k2, p4, k3, p3.
6th row: Sl 1 pw, k2, p3, k2, T2B, p2, k1, (C2B) twice, p6, k2, sl 1pw.
7th row: Sl 1pw, p2, k5, C2FP, p4, k3, p3, k3, p2, sl 1pw.
8th row: C3L, p3, k1, T2B, p3, k2, T2F, k1, C2B, p4, C3R.
9th row: P3, k3, C2FP, p3, k1, p2, k4, p2, k3, p3.
10th row: Sl 1 pw, k2, p3, T2B, p3, C2F, k1, p1, T2F, k3, p3, k2, sl 1pw.
11th row: Sl 1pw, p2, k3, p4, k2, p2, C2Bp, k7, p2, sl 1pw.
12th row: C3L, p6, (C2F) twice, k1, p2, T2F, k2, p3, C3R.
These 12 rows form the pattern.

MEASUREMENTS
Bust size: (77-82 (87-92, 107-112, 117-122, 127-132) cm (30-32 (34-36, 38-40, 42-44, 46-48, 50-52) in)
Garment size: 90 (101, 112, 123, 134, 145) cm (35.5 (39.75, 44, 48.5, 52.75, 57) in)
Length: 50 (52, 54, 56, 58, 60) cm (19.75 (20.5, 21.25, 22, 22.75, 23.5) in)
Instructions are given for the smallest size first, followed by the larger sizes in brackets.

NEEDLES & NOTIONS
One pair each of needles 3.25 mm (size 4), 3.75 mm (size 5) and 4 mm (size 6).
Cable needle
One large button or toggle to fasten

TENSION
Approx 22 sts x 28 rows = 10 cm (4 in) over st st on 4 mm (size 6) needles
Adjust needle size to give required tension

ABBREVIATIONS (see also page 140)
C2PB (cross 2 back purl-wise): slip next st onto a cable needle and hold at back of work, p1, then p1 from cable needle.
C2PF(cross 2 front purl-wise): slip next st onto a cable needle and hold at front of work, p1, then p1 from cable needle.
C2B (cross 2 back, knit-wise): slip next st onto a cable needle and hold at back of work, k1, then k1 from cable needle.
C2F (cross 2 front, knit-wise): slip next st onto a cable needle and hold at front of work, k1, then k1 from cable needle.
T2B (twist 2 back): slip next st onto a cable needle and hold at back of work, k1, then p1 from cable needle.
T2F (twist 2 front): slip next st onto a cable needle and hold at front of work, p1, then k1 from cable needle.
C3L (cable 3 left): slip next st onto a cable needle and hold at front of work, k2, then k1 from cable needle.
C3R (cable 3 right): slip next 2 sts onto a cable needle and hold at back of work, k1, then k2 from cable needle.

BACK (make 1)
Using 3.75 mm (size 5) needles cast on 106 (118, 130, 142, 154, 166) sts.
1st row: P2, (k2, p2) to end.
2nd row: K2, (p2, k2) to end.
These 2 rows form the rib.
Work a further 15 rows.

Change to 4 mm (size 6) needles.
1st row: (WS) K14 (18, 22, 26, 30, 34), work across 1st row of pattern panel, k26 (30, 34, 38, 42, 46) work across 1st row of pattern panel, k14 (18, 22, 26, 30, 34).
2nd row: P14 (18, 22, 26, 30, 34), work across 2nd row of pattern panel, p 26 (30, 34, 38, 42, 46) work across 2nd row of pattern panel, p 14 (18, 22, 26, 30, 34).
These 2 rows set cable panel with reversed st st between.

Continue in pattern until back measures 7 (7, 8, 8, 9, 9) cm (3 (3, 3½, 3½) in) from cast on edge, ending with a wrong side row.
Change back to 3.75 mm (US 5) needles to shapw waist. Work 18 rows. Change back to 4 mm (US 6) needles. Continue in pattern until back measures 30 (31, 32, 33, 34, 35) cm (11¾ (12¼, 12½, 13, 13¼, 13½) in) from cast on edge, ending with a wrong side row.

Shape armholes
Cast off 5 (6, 7, 8, 9, 10) sts at beginning of next 2 rows. 96 (106, 116, 126, 136, 146) sts.
Decrease one st at each end of the next and 7 (8, 9, 10, 11, 12) following alternate rows. 80 (88, 96, 104, 112, 120) sts.
Continue in pattern until back measures 50 (52, 54, 56, 58, 60) cm (19¾ (20½, 21¼, 22, 22¾, 23½) in) from cast on edge, ending with a wrong side row.

Shape shoulders
Cast off 8 (9, 10, 11, 12, 13) sts at beginning of next 6 rows.
Cast off remaining 32 (34, 36, 38, 40, 42) sts.

LEFT FRONT
(make 1)

Using 3.75 mm (US 5) needles cast on 49 (53, 61, 65, 73, 77) sts.
1st row: P2, (k2, p2) to last 3 sts, k3.
2nd row: P3, k2, (p2, k2) to end
Work a further 15 rows.

Change to 4 mm (US 6) needles.
1st row: (WS) K9 (9, 13, 13, 17, 17) work across 1st row of patt panel, k14 (18, 22, 26, 30, 34)
2nd row: P 14 (18, 22, 26, 30, 34), work across 2nd row of patt panel, p9 (9, 13, 13, 17, 17)
These rows set the cable panel with reversed st st between.
Continue in pattern until front measures 7 (7, 8, 8, 9, 9) cm

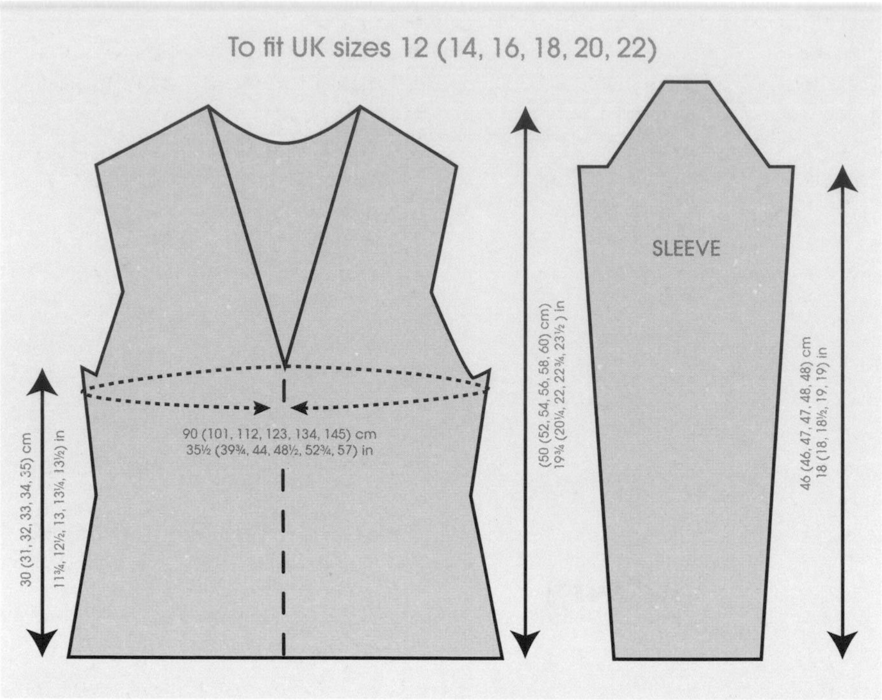

To fit UK sizes 12 (14, 16, 18, 20, 22)
SLEEVE
90 (101, 112, 123, 134, 145) cm
35½ (39¾, 44, 48½, 52¾, 57) in
30 (31, 32, 33, 34, 35) cm
11¾, 12½, 13, 13¼, 13½) in
(50 (52, 54, 56, 58, 60) cm)
19¾ (20¼, 22, 22¾, 23½) in
46 (46, 47, 47, 48, 48) cm
18 (18, 18½, 19, 19) in

(3 (3, 3½, 3½) in) from cast on edge, ending with wrong side row.

Change to 3.75 mm (US 5) needles. Work a further 18 rows.

Change back to 4 mm (US 6) needles. Continue in pattern until 12 rows less have been worked than on back to armhole shaping, ending with a wrong side row.

Shape neck
Next row: pattern to last 2 sts, work 2 tog.
Work 3 rows.
Rep the last 4 rows 3 times more. 45 (49, 57, 61, 69, 73) sts.
Shape armhole
Next row: Cast off 5 (6, 7, 8, 9, 10) sts, pattern to last 2 sts work 2 tog. 39 (42, 49, 52, 59, 62) sts.
Work 1 row.
Continue to decrease at neck edge on every 4th row **at the same time** decrease one st at armhole edge of the next and 7 (8, 9, 10, 11, 12) following alternate rows.
Keeping armhole edge straight continue to decrease at neck edge on every 4th row until 24 (27, 30, 33, 36, 39) sts remain.
Work straight until front measures same as back to shoulder, ending at armhole edge.

Shape shoulder
Cast off 8 (9, 10, 11, 12, 13) sts at beginning of next and following alternate row.
Work 1 row. Cast off remaining 8(9, 10, 11, 12, 13) sts.

RIGHT FRONT (make 1)

Using 3.75 mm (size 5) needles cast on 49 (53, 61, 65, 73, 77) sts.
1st row: K3, p2, (k2, p2) to end.
2nd row: K2, (p2, k2) to last 3 sts, p3.
Work a further 15 rows in rib.
Change to 4 mm (size 6) needles.
1st row: (WS) K14 (18, 22, 26, 30, 34) work across 1st row of patt panel, k9 (9, 13, 13, 17, 17).
2nd row: P9 (9, 13, 13, 17, 17), work across 2nd row of patt panel, p14 (18, 22, 26, 30, 34).
These 2 rows set the cable panel with reversed st st between. Continue in pattern until front measures 7 (7, 8, 8, 9, 9) cm (3 (3, 3½, 3½) in) from cast

on edge, ending with a wrong side row.
Change to 3.75 mm (size 5) needles. Work a further 18 rows. Change to 4 mm (size 6) needles. Continue in pattern until 12 rows fewer have been worked than on back to armhole shaping, ending with a wrong side row.

Shape neck
Next row: Work 2tog, pattern to end. Work 3 rows.
Rep the last 4 rows 3 times more.
Next row: Work 2tog, pattern to end, leaving 44 (48, 56, 60, 68, 72) sts.
Shape armhole
Next row: Cast off 5(6, 7, 8, 9, 10) sts, pattern to end. 39 (42, 49, 52, 59, 62) sts.
Continue to decrease at neck edge on every 4th row **and at the same time** decrease 1st at armhole edge of the next and 7 (8, 9, 10, 11, 12) following alternate rows.
Keeping armhole edge straight continue to decrease at neck edge on every 4th row until 24 (27, 30, 33, 36, 39) sts remain. Work straight until front measures the same as back to shoulder, ending at armhole edge.

Shape shoulder
Cast off 8 (9, 10, 11, 12, 13) sts at beginning of next and following alternate row.
Work 1 row.
Cast off remaining 8 (9, 10, 11, 12, 13) sts.

SLEEVES (make 2)
Using size 3 (3.25 mm) needles cast on 38 (42, 46, 50, 54, 58) sts.

1st, 3rd and 5th sizes only
1st row: P2, (k2, p2) to end.
2nd row: K2, (p2, k2) to end.

2nd, 4th and 6th sizes only
1st row: K2, (p2, k2) to end.
2nd row: P2, (k2, p2) to end.

All sizes
These 2 rows form the rib. Work a further 15 rows. Change to 4 mm (size 6) needles.
1st row: (WS) K6 (8, 10, 12, 14, 16), work across 1st row of patt panel, k6 (8, 10, 12, 14, 16).
2nd row: P6 (8, 10, 12, 14, 16), work across 2nd row of patt panel, p6 (8, 10, 12, 14, 16).

These 2 rows set the cable panel with reversed st st between. Work 5 rows.
Increase row P3, m1, patt to last 3 sts, m1, p3.
Repeat the last 6 rows 17 times more. 74 (78, 82, 86, 90, 94) sts.

Continue straight until sleeve measures 46 (46, 47, 47, 48, 48) cm (18 (18, 18½, 18½, 19, 19) in) from cast on edge, ending with wrong side row.

Shape top
Cast off 5 (6, 7, 8, 9, 10) sts at beginning of next 2 rows. 64 (66, 68, 70, 72, 74) sts.
Work 0 (2, 0, 2, 0, 2) rows.
1st row: pattern to end.
2nd row: pattern to end.
3rd row: Work 2 tog, pattern to last 2sts, work 2tog.
4th row: pattern to end.
Repeat the last 4 rows 3 (3, 4, 4, 5, 5) times more, to make 56 (58, 58, 60, 60, 62) sts.
Cast off 4 sts at beginning of next 12 rows, leaving 8 (10, 10, 12, 12, 14) sts. Cast off .

LEFT FRONT BAND and COLLAR (make 1)
Using size 3 (3.25 mm) needles, and with right side facing, cast on 22 (22, 26, 26, 30, 30) sts, pick up and k 54 (56, 58, 60, 62, 64) sts to beginning of neck shaping, 58 (60, 62, 64, 66, 68) sts to cast on edge. 134 (138, 146, 150, 158, 162) sts in total.
1st row: P2, (k2, p2) to end. This row sets the rib.
Next 2 rows: Rib 22 (22, 26, 26, 30, 30) turn, rib to end.

Next 2 rows: Rib 26 (26, 30, 30, 34, 34) turn, rib to end.
Next 2 rows: Rib 30 (30, 34, 34, 38, 38) turn, rib to end.
Next 2 rows: Rib 34 (34, 38, 38, 42, 42) turn, rib to end.
Next 2 rows: Rib 38 (38, 42, 42, 46, 46) turn, rib to end.
Continue in this way working 4 extra sts on every alternate row until row rib 74 (74, 82, 82, 90, 90) turn, rib to end, has been worked.
Rib 12 (12, 12, 14, 14, 14) rows across all sts. Cast off in rib.

RIGHT FRONT BAND (make 1)
Using size 3 (3.25 mm) needles, and with RS facing, pick up and k 58 (60, 62, 64, 66, 68) sts to beginning of neck shaping, 54 (56, 58, 60, 62, 64) sts to shoulder seam, cast on 22 (22, 26, 26, 30, 30) sts, to make a total of 134 (138, 146, 150, 158, 162) sts.
Work in p2, k2 rib as follows:
Next 2 rows: Rib 22 (22, 26, 26, 30, 30) turn, rib to end.
Next 2 rows: Rib 26 (26, 30, 30, 34, 34) turn, rib to end.
Next 2 rows: Rib 30 (30, 34, 34, 38, 38) turn, rib to end.
Next 2 rows: Rib 34 (34, 38, 38, 42, 42) turn, rib to end.
Next 2 rows: Rib 38 (38, 42, 42, 46, 46) turn, rib to end.
Continue in this way working 4 extra sts on every alternate row until the row rib 74 (74, 82, 82, 90, 90) turn, rib to end, has been worked. Rib 5 rows across all sts.
1st buttonhole row: Rib 50 (52, 54, 56, 58, 60), cast off 3 sts, rib to end.
2nd buttonhole row: Rib, casting on 3 sts over those cast off.
Work 5 (5, 5, 7, 7, 7) rows across all sts. Cast off in rib.

MAKE UP
Join collar row ends. Sew collar to back neck. Join side and sleeve seams. Sew in sleeves. Sew on button.

pure wool
practicals

Yarn selector

What makes a good quality knitting yarn? Generally, we want finer and softer fleeces as these are more comfortable. However, do not ignore the character of the wool – it is unreasonable to expect even the very finest Hebridean to be as fine as the finest Shetland, so this must also be taken into account.

A healthy sheep will produce better wool, irrespective of all other factors, so this is the most important starting point. Sheep who are well cared for, living in an environment appropriate for their breed and age, will produce good wool. Then many more specific factors that relate to the individual sheep come in to play.

Breed

Genetics affects wool in two ways: the genes of the breed (Black Welsh Mountain is very different from Cotswold, for example), and the genes of an individual animal (some Black Welsh Mountain sheep have coarser, or darker, or crimpier fleeces than others within a flock).

These factors become even more pronounced with mules and other cross-bred sheep, and are also characteristic of primitive sheep: North Ronaldsay, Gotland and Shetland are more varied in colour and fleece style than other sheep.

Generally, darker wools are coarser and paler, and coloured wools are finer,

BREED	Rarity	Staple length	Fleece weight	Micron	Lustre	Fibre type
BLACK WELSH MOUNTAIN	native	6–10 cm (3–4 in)	1.25–2 kg (3–4 lbs)	32–35	no	medium
BLUE-FACED LEICESTER	not rare	6–15 cm (3–6 in)	1–2 kg (2–4 lbs)	26–26.5	semi	fine
CASTLEMILK MOORIT	vulnerable	5–8 cm (2–3 in)	1 kg (2.2 lbs)	30–31.5	no	fine
CORRIEDALE/FALKLANDS	not rare	7.5–12.5 cm (3–5 in)	4.5–6 kg (10–13 lbs)	26–33	no	fine
COTSWOLD	at risk	17.5–30 cm (7–12 in)	4–7 kg (9–15 lbs)	34–40	yes	medium
GALWAY	rare	11–19 cm (4.5–7.5 in)	2.5–3.5 kg (5.5–7.7lbs)	30	semi	medium
GOTLAND	rare in UK	6–12 cm (3–5 in)	1–4 kg (2–8 lbs)	28–32	yes	medium
HEBRIDEAN	native	5–15 cm (2–6 in)	1–2 kg (2–4 lbs)	35+	some	strong
HERDWICK	vulnerable	5–10 cm (2–4 in)	1.5–2 kg (2–4 lbs)	35+	no	strong
JACOB	native	6–15 cm (3–6 in)	1.75–2.75 kg (3–5 lbs)	28–35	no	medium
MANX LOAGTHAN	at risk	7–10 cm (2.5–4 in)	1–2 kg (2–4 lbs)	30	no	medium
NORTH RONALDSAY	endangered	4–8 cm (1.5–3 in)	1–2 kg (2–4 lbs)	25–40	no	medium
ROMNEY	not rare	10–17 cm (4–7 in)	3–5 kg (7–11 lbs)	30–34	yes	medium
RYELAND	native	7.5–10 cm (3–4 in)	2–2.75 kg (4–5 lbs)	28–32	no	medium
SHETLAND	native	5–10 cm (2–4 in)	1 kg (2.2 lbs)	12–30	no	fine
ZWARTBLES	rare in UK	10–12.5 cm (4–5 in)	2–3 kg (4–6.5lbs)	31–34	no	medium

Wool Characteristics and Yarn Types

across and within breeds and, in the case of Jacob sheep, sometimes even on the same sheep!

Rams usually have coarser coats than ewes, and wethers tend to keep lamb characteristics, so their fleeces are more like those of ewes than rams.

Age

Young sheep have finer fleeces, with lambs and shearlings being the best. As sheep get older they produce coarser fleeces. However, some older sheep have fine fleeces because of their genetics, and it is by no means a rule that a lamb will have finer wool than a ewe of the same breed.

The fleeces of each breed are very different to look at and feel – and remember that feeling the soft wool on a sheep's back, or just after shearing, is feeling it at its best. Once we process and twist the wool into yarns it becomes harder. This is why a soft, fine wool such as Gotland may not feel as soft when in a ball but, with washing and wearing, will gradually soften.

Wools that tend to felt will soften more with age than those that are less easy to

The table below summarises the characteristics of the breeds we have covered in this book, and shows the most appropriate yarns we think they will make. It includes whether woollen or worsted yarns are preferable, whether blending is useful, and what fibres can be usefully blended with the basic wool of particular breeds. Where a wool is either very rare or pretty good as it is, we have suggested leaving well alone! But some that are nice, but less rare, are worth experimenting with to get more variety, while others benefit by becoming softer or better by blending. Adding mohair to darker wools increases softness and produces a better result from dyeing. Adding a small amount of coloured wool to a white wool adds interest and a more subtle effect with dyeing.

Handle	Lace	4-ply Sportweight	DK Worsted	Aran Medium	Chunky Bulky	Gurnsey	Other possible yarns	Better Worsted	Better Woollen	Good Blended	Purpose of blend	Blend suggestions
soft			●	●	●		4-ply	no	yes	yes		
soft		●	●				aran, chunky	either	either	possible	variety	silk, flax
medium			●	●			chunky		yes	yes	improve	silk, alpaca
soft		●	●	●	●			either	either	possible	variety	silk, flax, Manx Loagthan, Hebridean, Black Welsh Mountain
medium			●	●			4-ply, chunky	yes	no	no		
medium				●	●	●	DK	either	either	no		
soft		●	●	●			lace, chunky	no	yes	possible	variety	silk, Merino, Corriedale
strong			●	●	●		4-ply	no	yes	yes	improve	Manx Loagthan, mohair
strong				●	●		DK	no	yes	yes	improve	mohair
medium			●	●	●	●	4-ply	either	either	yes	variety	mohair, alpaca
medium			●	●			chunky, guernsey	no	yes	yes	improve	Hebridean, mohair
medium			●	●	●			no	yes	no		
medium			●	●		●	chunky	either	either	possible	variety	Manx Loagthan, Hebridean
medium			●	●	●		4-ply	no	yes	yes	variety	coloured Ryeland
soft	●	●	●				aran	no	yes	yes	variety	coloured Shetland
medium			●	●	●	●	4-ply	no	yes	yes	improve	mohair, alpaca

felt, and worsted-spun yarns will felt less than woollen-spun yarns. Similarly, a lustre yarn will produce a different appearance and feel smoother, even if coarser, than a non-lustre yarn.

Some yarns, though, are naturally very soft, these include Corriedale and Shetland, even though they have no lustre.

But this is only the beginning, as yarns from each breed have individual characteristics. As the *Wool Qualities and Yarn Types* chart (below) shows, soft wools do not necessarily make fine or drapey yarns, and coarse wools do not inevitably have to be consigned to the Aran section. Also a lustre wool will be considerably denser than a non-lustre, so will make very heavy garments if used as a worsted-spun yarn, in chunky weight, or for larger items. In fact, it is better to use woollen-spun, semi-lustre, or non-lustre yarns for these.

The patterns in this book have been designed with a view to the most suitable projects. If you have a similar pattern it will probably work in the yarn we have chosen. For example, many accessories such as scarves and mittens, as well as cushions, will work in plenty of different yarns from several breeds.

Wool Qualities and Yarn Types

BREED	Micron	Lustre	Fibre type	Handle	Lace	4-ply / Sportweight	DK / Worsted	Aran / Medium	Chunky / Bulky	Gurnsey
HERDWICK	35+	no	strong	strong						
HEBRIDEAN	35+	some	strong	strong						
COTSWOLD	34–40	yes	medium	medium						
BLACK WELSH MOUNTAIN	32–35	no	medium	soft						
NORTH RONALDSAY	25–40	no	medium	medium						
ZWARTBLES	31–34	no	medium	medium						
GALWAY	30+	semi	medium	medium						
MANX LOAGHTAN	30+	no	medium	medium						
ROMNEY	30–34	yes	medium	medium						
CASTLEMILK MOORIT	30–31.5	no	fine	medium						
RYELAND	28–32	no	medium	medium						
JACOB	28–35	no	medium	medium						
GOTLAND	28–32	yes	medium	soft						
CORRIEDALE/FALKLANDS	26–33	no	fine	soft						
BLUE-FACED LEICESTER	26–26.5	semi	fine	soft						
SHETLAND	12–30	no	fine	soft						

The chart above lists the wools in order of the micron count rather than alphabetically, so that the gradual change in suitability of yarns from fine to thicker can be seen more clearly.

The dark shading shows the first choice of appropriate yarns for the particular wool.

The pale shading gives possible options, either with the help of a bit of alpaca or mohair, or by choosing finer fleeces.

Substitutions

If you choose a different breed of sheep for a project, bear in mind the appropriate yarn ranges shown in Wool Qualities and Yarn Types (see page 134). For example, it will not work as well to make an Aran pattern in a yarn such as Blue-faced Leicester or Shetland, or to make a 4-ply pattern from a yarn such as Manx Loagthan or Romney (unless they have been blended with a fibre to help the yarn work better). However, if you choose a project such as the Scallop Shell Top (see page 28), which needs lustre and definition, and want an alternative to Blue-faced Leicester (it is nice in an alpaca yarn, by the way), it will not work as well in Corriedale, which has no lustre, or in Gotland, which felts with wear.

Some of the designs in the book are very specific to the breed of sheep and the wool it produces. The most obvious case is the Shetland Fair Isle waistcoat (see page 118), although this could, at a push, be done with natural and dyed Jacob (not so soft though) or with North Ronaldsay (a different shading and texture so less distinct, which would make the design fuzzy).

It is a relatively safe bet to use a Jacob yarn for most knitting patterns, and the designs for Jacob yarns included

Better Worsted	Better Woollen	Good for	Bad for	Key characteristics in yarn
no	yes	accessories	next to skin	Coarse, kempy but great heathered colours
no	yes	accessories	next to skin	A good dark off-black, strong, lambs can be very soft, slight lustre in lambs
yes	no	near skin	detail/cable	Strong, lustrous, and creamy with ideal long staple for worsted, lambs fine
no	yes	near skin	detail/cable	Soft and a good dark almost black, versatile
no	yes	outerwear	detail/cable	Double coat, fine and coarse, feels reasonably soft, good natural colour range
either	yes	outerwear	detail/cable	Nice bouncy, off-black, good general option between Hebridean and Black Welsh Mountain
no	either	near skin		Good general purpose medium, semi-lustre yarn, some dark hairs add interest
either	yes	outerwear		Brown, bouncy, short, bulky, if long enough can be worsted-spun
no	either	near skin		Nice creamy yarn, long enough for worsted, good mixed and all-rounder
no	yes	near skin	hard wear	Rare, short and needs a bit of help, but OK for pure blends in thicker yarns
either	yes	outerwear		Nice bouncy, reasonably soft wool, two good colours to mix and match
maybe	either	near skin		Very versatile in colour range, good work-horse alone and blends and dyes well
either	yes	near skin	detail/cable	True grey, lustre, long, can pill and shed in worsted due to smooth fibres working out, dyes beautifully
either	either	next to skin	hard wear	Very white, soft, bulky, versatile, dyes well, will blend well to add interest
no	either	next to skin	outerwear	Lovely creamy, soft semi-lustre, can feel a bit spongy when soft worsted-spun
no	yes	next to skin	accessories	Every natural colour, soft and very fine, will blend with alpaca for smoothness and brighter natural colours

• Corriedale and Blue-faced Leicester are both soft and fine, but the first is bulky and the second is lean so use Corriedale for warmth and Blue-faced Leicester for drape.

• The long lustre wools do not make good chunky yarns as they are dense, so the yarns become heavy if made thick – this is also the case with alpaca.

• Wensleydale would be better than Cotswold for 4-ply and lace-weight and is similar in style.

• North Ronaldsay makes a soft 4-ply if de-haired of its coarse hairs but loses its character – better to use Shetland.

• Near skin means people able to wear wool should be able to wear this next to skin, but others will need something between them and the wool!

• For bulk and warmth use: Black Welsh Mountain, North Ronaldsay, Manx Loagthan, Ryeland, Corriedale/Falkland, Shetland.

• For drape and sheen use: Cotswold, Gotland, Blue-faced Leicester.

• For intermediate or individual use: Herdwick, Hebridean, Zwartbles, Galway, Romney, Castlemilk Moorit, Jacob.

It is a relatively safe bet to use a Jacob yarn for most knitting patterns, and the designs for Jacob yarns included in this book will work in many different breed yarns because Jacob is such a versatile wool. In fact, once you blend Jacob with mohair – and if you dye it as well – you could probably spend the rest of your life without knitting with another breed, unless you want to make lace!

Gauge

This is all useful, **BUT it is vitally important to remember that if you need the measurements of your work to be exact you MUST make a gauge swatch – the bigger the better – as it will also illustrate the drape and handle of the resulting fabric.** If you just pin it out very slightly stretched on a cushion to count the stitches and rows, and do not wash and press it, it will be sufficiently accurate, and you just rip it back to use in your main project.

It is a relatively complex exercise to grade a pattern made for a 4-ply yarn for a Double Knitting or thicker yarn, and vice-versa, so it is much better to get the correct yarn weight for your project. A useful rule of thumb is that, with Blacker Yarns (but not all yarns!),

Matching yarns to patterns

Remember you will need to change the yarn or re-scale the pattern if you try some of the other options

Breed	Main pattern	Yarn UK name	Cozy body-warmer	Scallop shell top	Baby's log cabin blanket	Cable and rib sweater	Hot-water bottle cover	Wavy cable jumper
BLACK WELSH MOUNTAIN	Cozy body-warmer	DK	■					
BLUE-FACED LEICESTER	Scallop shell top	DK		■	▨		░	
BLUE-FACED LEICESTER	Baby's log cabin blanket	DK			■	▨		
CASTLEMILK MOORIT	Cable and rib sweater	DK				■		
CORRIEDALE/FALKLANDS	Hot-water bottle cover	2 x DK				▨	■	
COTSWOLD	Wavy cable jumper	DK					░	■
GALWAY	Pucker cable tunic	Aran	▨					
GOTLAND	Long cardigan with pockets	DK	░					▨
GOTLAND	Autumn leaves beret	4-ply						
HEBRIDEAN	Hebridean handbag	2 x Aran	▨					
HEBRIDEAN	Sanquhar cushion	DK	░					
HERDWICK	Tea, cafetière and egg cosies	Aran	▨					
JACOB	Jacob cable jacket	2 x DK	▨			▨	▨	
JACOB/MOHAIR*	Socks for walking and welly boots	4 x and Aran	░					▨
MANX LOAGTHAN	Zig-zag scarf, hat and mittens	DK	▨					
NORTH RONALDSAY	Airy waistcoat	Aran	▨					
ROMNEY	Traditional Guernsey pullover	Guernsey	▨					
RYELAND	Ryeland child's hooded jacket	2 x DK	▨					
SHETLAND	Shetland spot waistcoat	4-ply					▨	
SHETLAND	Shetland feather and fan scarf	DK					░	
ZWARTBLES	Climbing vine cardigan	DK	▨					

SUMMARY FOR BREED SPECIFIC YARNS

- ■ Breed yarn for pattern
- ▨ Breed yarns possible for pattern
- ░ Breed yarns borderline for pattern
- ☐ Breed yarns not recommended for pattern

* for Jacob/mohair, other blends with mohair such as Manx, Hebridean and Zwartbles would also be appropriate

two strands of 4-ply are equivalent to Aran and two strands of Double Knitting are equivalent to Chunky.

Needle size

You can enlarge a design simply by knitting it in a thicker yarn on larger needles, or reduce it by using a thinner yarn and smaller needles. Again you should make a gauge swatch to work out how much larger or smaller your project will be. Once you know how many stitches make up 10 cm or 4 in, you can work out from the pattern (use the back or the maximum number of stitches if in the round) how many inches or centimeters you will create by casting on the stitches specified for each size. Therefore you will know how much larger or smaller your own project will be.

Care advice

Hand-wash pure wool in cool water using a liquid wool wash. You can spin the knitted garment but do not tumble dry. Instead, spread on a towel, hand-pressing it into shape and to the correct size and leave to dry. Store folded. If a garment requires ironing, press on the wrong side when almost dry. Do not iron ribbing.

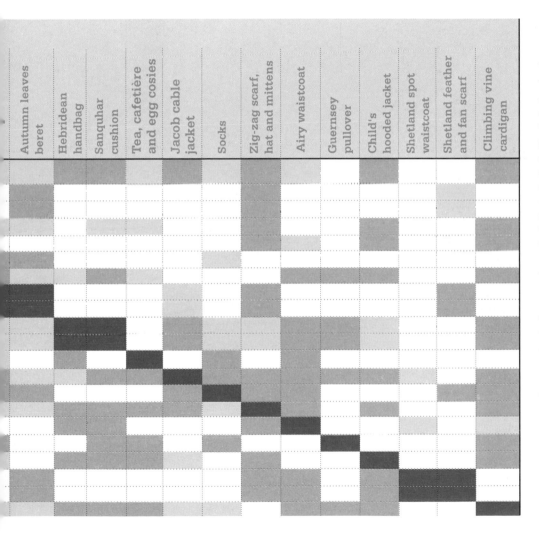

The chart left shows the patterns we have designed as most appropriate for each yarn in the darkest shade, with a range of paler and palest shades. You should obtain a satisfactory result in the paler shade, but may be taking wool and yarn too far from its natural preference in the palest shades. We have used UK yarn names, as these are the recommended yarns; US equivalents are shown on *Wool Qualities and Yarn Types* (see page 134) and *Yarn Terminology* (page 16).

Dyeing pure wool

Weaving and crochet are beyond the scope of this book, but here is a small introduction to dyeing. Dyeing is like cookery – it can be very creative and satisfying, but as you are dealing with natural materials it can also be variable!

Wool (such as mohair, silk and alpaca) is a fibre made of protein, so it will dye differently to cotton, hemp or flax, which are vegetable, or artificial fibres, which are mineral. However, different wool fibres will dye differently, so it is possible to put, say, Galway, Romney and White Ryeland into the same dye at the same time, and they will all come out slightly differently (if blue, of course they will all be blue, but the blues will differ!).

We recommend only dyeing some of your yarn and using it with the natural colours to enhance them – many patterns in this book work well with a welt and cuffs in a darker or brighter colour, or with stripes.

If you are intending to use only dyed yarn, take note of the comments in *Wool Qualities and Yarn Types* (see page 134) and remember that dyeing coloured yarn will leave the natural colour as the base and not white!

If you wish to mix dyed and naturally coloured yarns in a project, avoid primary colours as these can clash. However, red and yellow work with dark natural wools, and blue works with white or brown (when it will seem grey). To achieve these contrasts, dye white wool.

Key points:
• Dye wool in LOOSELY tied hanks: if tied tightly the dye cannot reach all of the wool and it will be patchy.

Wool Colours and Dye Ideas

BREED	MAIN COLOUR	Off-black	Dark brown	Brown grey	Mid-brown	Fawn	Creamy white	Ivory white	White	Pale grey	Mid-grey	Dark grey
BLACK WELSH MOUNTAIN	black	■	■	■			▨					
BLUE-FACED LEICESTER	creamy white						▨					
CASTLEMILK MOORIT	mid-brown				■							
CORRIEDALE/FALKLANDS	very white								☐			
COTSWOLD	creamy white						▨					
GALWAY	ivory white											
GOTLAND	grey									▨	■	■
HEBRIDEAN	black	■	■	■								
HERDWICK	multi					▨			☐		■	■
JACOB	mid-grey	■	■	■		▨			☐			
MANX LOAGHTAN	mid-brown				■							
NORTH RONALDSAY	multi		■							▨	■	■
ROMNEY	milk white											
RYELAND	multi					■					■	■
SHETLAND	multi	■	■	■	■	▨	▨		☐		■	■
ZWARTBLES	black	■	■						☐			

- Wash the wool well beforehand: any residual grease will make the result patchy.
- The wool must be evenly and completely wetted without trapped air: otherwise it will be patchy.
- Bring the wool and dye to boiling point to activate the chemicals. DO NOT agitate it as this could cause felting.
- Different dyes work at different temperatures, so it is important to raise the temperature SLOWLY or there is risk of patchiness or colour variation.
- If you want to repeat a colour, measure and work accurately and write down what you do, keeping a sample of each dye-lot.
- Glass, enamel or stainless steel utensils work best – aluminium, copper and iron may react with the dyes.
- Cover yourself, your floor and your work surfaces to protect them from the dye.
- Some dyestuffs are poisonous, so you should wear gloves, protective glasses and a face mask when dealing with very fine powders in particular.
- Dyes need auxiliary chemicals to help them work, usually to neutralise or acidify the water – most wool dyes require acid conditions to fix them and the dye bonds chemically with the fibre, so your dye-bath should be almost colourless when you have finished (if it is not, you can re-use it to dye something a paler colour).

A simple dye to try is the drink Kool Aid (we wonder what colour our insides become if we drink it). Also cold tea works well for a brown, but these are effectively dyeing by staining rather than by chemicals.

Many vegetable dyes vary from batch to batch so it is worth a trial first. Some of these fade fast in daylight – although strong sunlight will bleach everything, including dark naturally coloured wools (which is why they are usually off-black). There are many excellent books on dyeing and growing plants to make dyes, so even if you are unable to grow your own wool you can add a little home-grown personality to your yarns.

DYE IDEAS	NOTES AND SUGGESTIONS
no	could dye blue, purple, or red to alter off-black
any pastel	remember the golden base will affect the dyed result!
red, gold, brown	the brown can be a bit dull, but it's rare, so better natural
any bright	can look a bit artificial when dyed, unless blended
any pastel or bright	good for dyeing due to lustre, but cream base will affect dyed result a bit
any pastel	as this is rare, I would probably leave it natural
blue, wine, purple, olive, gold	lovely heathered shades when dyed, with great depth
no	could dye blue, purple, or red to alter off-black
blue, wine, purple, olive, gold	lovely heathered shades when dyed, with great depth
blue, wine, purple, olive, gold	a good base for experimenting with plain and heathered shades
red, gold, brown	better to blend with mohair and then dye, probably
blue, wine, purple, olive, gold	rare and nice as it is, would not bother to dye!
any pastel	some natural and some with, say, olive or denim blue, for two-colour designs
blue, wine, purple, olive, gold	the coloured is very nice undyed, so probably better to use Jacob!
no	lovely as it is, would not bother to dye!
no	could dye blue, purple, or red to alter off-black

Knitting know-how

On the following pages you will find information about the abbreviations and technical terms used in the patterns in this book, plus advice on making-up and caring for your pure wool knitwear.

Abbreviations

Alt: alternate.

Dec (Decrease): Knit or purl 2 stitches together, or s1, k1, psso on knit rows and p2togtbl on purl rows.

DPN: Double Pointed Needles.

Inc (Increase): Knit or purl into both the front and back of a st, to create 2 stitches.

k: knit.

K2tog or P2tog: knit or purl the next 2 stitches together.

k2togtbl: knit two stitches together through the back of the loop (rather than the front).

K3tog or P3tog: knit or purl the next 3 stitches together.

K tbl: through back loop.

Kw: knitwise.

m1 (make one): pick up loop between st just worked and next st and knit into back of loop.

p: purl.

p2togtbl: purl two stitches together through the back of the loop (rather than the front).

psso: pass the slipped st over the next knitted st.

Pw: purlwise.

RS: right side.

sl: slip a st from one needle to the other.

st. st: stocking stitch.

st, sts: stitch, stitches.

SM: stitch marker.

Tog: together.

Tw2: twist 2 stitches – take the needle past the first st knit into second st, then knit first st, slip both stitches off the needle together.

WS: wrong side.

yf: (yarn forward, sometimes called 'yarn over'). Pass the yarn over the needle between two stitches, making a loop, which you knit or purl into in the next row to create an extra st.

Stitches

Garter stitch: knit every row.

Stocking stitch: Row 1 (RS): knit to end; Row 2 (WS): purl to end; repeat these 2 rows.

Reverse stocking stitch: Row 1 (RS): purl to end; Row 2 (WS): knit to end; repeat these 2 rows.

Moss stitch: alternate rows of k1, p1, so the knit stitches are over the purl stitches on the previous row.

Seed stitch: another name for moss stitch.

2 x 2 rib: Row 1: (k2, p2) repeat to end. Row 2: (p2, k2) repeat to end. Repeat these rows for the required number of rows or the required length is reached.

English, Continental or long-tail cast-on: Unwind 2.5 cm (1 in) yarn for each st, plus a tail. Make a slip knot at this point in the yarn and place it on needle in your right hand. Hold length of yarn in your left hand. Pass it around your left thumb and hold in against the palm of your hand with your fourth and fifth fingers. Insert point of needle into loop around your thumb. Bring yarn from ball around needle and draw it through loop around your thumb to create a st on the needle, slipping loop off your thumb as you do so. Tighten st on needle and make a new loop around your thumb ready for next st.

Cable cast-on: Make a slip knot and place it on the needle in your left hand. With the yarn and second needle in your right hand, insert tip of right-hand needle into the loop on the left-hand needle and pass the yarn around the tip. Use the tip to pull the yarn through and place the loop you have created onto the left-hand needle to make second st. To make the third, and all subsequent stitches, insert the tip of the right-hand needle between the first and second stitches and knit a st between them.

Magic loop

This method allows you to knit in the round using one long circular needle instead of a set of DPNs. Cast on and slide stitches onto the cable. Find the centre of the row and pull the cable through at this point to make a large loop. Arrange stitches so half are on each needle. Both needles should point in the same direction and the last stitches worked should be at the rear. Move rear-needle stitches to cable and knit stitches on front needle. There will be a loop of cable at both sides of work. When you have worked all stitches on front needle (half the round), slip rear-needle stitches back onto needle and turn your work. Repeat steps 3 and 4 as required.

Making-up tips

Blocking: Darn in all ends and then wash all pieces. Gently squeeze out excess water and then, on a flat surface padded with towels, pin out the pieces to the dimensions given in the pattern and leave until dry. Alternatively, pin out the dry, unwashed knitting and spray with water, then leave to dry. Or, press on the wrong side using a steam iron (pad the ironing board with a towel). **Joning seams:** generally a simple backstitch is ideal for this. However, for a 'hidden' seam, use **Mattress stitch**: place both pieces on a flat surface, side-by-side and with right sides facing. Attach yarn to right-hand side and bring needle to front between first and second stitches of first row. Take thread under loop between first and second stitches of first row on left-hand side of seam. Repeat on right-hand side. Continue to complete seam.

Finishing sock toes: Kitchener stitch creates an invisible seam at the toe of a sock. Using a large needle and spare yarn, or the tail from the end of the stitches on the back needle, and holding together two needles in parallel with an equal number of stitches on each, start by bringing the yarn through the first st on the front needle as if to purl, leaving the st on the needle. Take the yarn through the corresponding back st as if to knit, again leaving that st on the needle. *Bring the yarn back and through the same front st as already threaded, but this time as if to knit and slip this st off the needle. Next take the yarn through the next front st as if to purl, again leaving the st on the needle and then go to the first back st and bring the needle through as if to purl and slip that st off, then through the next back st as if to knit, leaving it on the needle.* Now repeat from * to * until all the stitches are used.

Decorations

To make **tassels**, wind yarn around a piece of card then cut along one edge to create even lengths. For the tea and cafetière cosies (see page 78) we used card 10 cm (4 in) wide; for the egg cosies 5 cm (2 in) wide. Take six lengths for small tassels and 20 for large ones, fold in half and tie yarn tightly around the centre, leaving ends long enough to sew onto the item. Bend lengths back together and wind a piece of yarn around the bunch several times 1 cm (0.5 in) from tied fold.

To make **pom-poms**, cut out two discs of card, each with a central hole. For the tea and cafetière cosies (see page 78) we used a diameter of 10 cm (4 in) and a hole of 2 cm (0.75 in). For the egg cosies, a diameter of 6.5 cm (2.5 in) and a hole of 1.5 cm (0.7 in). For the beanies (see page 92) a diameter of 8 cm (3 in) and hole of 2 cm (0.75 in). Using a darning needle, and with the disks held together, wind a doubled length of yarn around them until they are well covered. Slip the point of a pair of scissors between the wool and discs and cut around the edge. Pull the discs slightly apart, leaving the ends caught, and wind yarn very tightly around threads between the discs and tie securely, leaving long ends. Slide off the discs.

Bibliography

This is a personal choice of a few books that have inspired, informed and challenged me, and that focus on specific breeds and some knitting techniques and designs. I am an avid collector of knitting books, so this selection was difficult to make – some of the books may only be available secondhand, but I think they will be worth seeking out. I hope you find these books as interesting as I do!

BOOKS ABOUT SHEEP, SPINNING, FLEECE, AND FIBRE

Robson, Deborah, and Ekarius, Carol, *The Fleece and Fibre Sourcebook* (Storey Publishing, 2011)

Fournier, Nola and Jane, *In Sheep's Clothing: A Handspinners Guide to Wool* (Interweave Press, 2003)

Jackson, Constance, and Plowman, Judith, *The Woolcraft Book: Spinning, Weaving, Dyeing* (Collins/ Scribner, 1982)

British Wool Marketing Board, *British Sheep & Wool, A Guide to British Sheep Breeds and Their Unique Wool* (British Wool Marketing Board, 2010)

Jenkins, J. Geraint, *From Fleece to Fabric: The technological history of the Welsh Woollen Industry* (Gomer, 1981)

Davies, John William, *Welsh Sheep and Their Wool* (Gomer, 1981)

Jenkins, J. Geraint, Drefach and the Woollen Industry (Gomer, 1981)

Teal, Peter, *Hand Woolcombing and Spinning, A Guide to Worsteds from the Spinning-Wheel* (Blandford Press, 1985)

Buchanan, Rita, *A Dyer's Garden* (Interweave Press, 1995)

BOOKS ABOUT KNITTING

Crompton, Claire, *The Knitter's Bible* (David & Charles, 2004)

Walker, Barbara G., A Treasury of Knitting Patterns (Schoolhouse Press, 1998) (See also pretty much anything by this great woman! This includes her second, third and fourth books of knitting patterns, including charts, and also *Knitting from the Top*.)

Thomas, Mary, *Mary Thomas's Book of Knitting Patterns* (Dover, 1972)

Rutt, Richard, *A History of Handknitting* (Batsford, 1987) (Now out of print but also published by Interweave Press)

Zimmerman, Elizabeth, *Knitting without Tears* (Simon & Shuster, 1973)

Zimmerman, Elizabeth, *Knitter's Almanac* (Dover, 1982)

Foale, Marion, *Classic Knitwear* (Rodale Press, 1985)

Gibson, Priscilla A, and Robson, Deborah, *Knitting in the Old Way* (Nomad Press, 2004)

Wright, Mary, *Cornish Guernseys and Knit-frocks* (Alison Hodge/Ethnographica, 2008)

Kagan, Sasha, *Big and Little Sweaters* (Dorling Kindersley, 1987)

Starmore, Alice, *Aran Knitting* (Dover, 1999)

Starmore, Alice, *Fair Isle Knitting* (Taunton Press, 1993)

Starmore, Alice, *Fisherman's Sweaters* (Collins & Brown, 1994)

Interweave Press produces many useful books, and among my favourites are *Folk Vests* by Cheryl Oberle, *Folk Socks* by Nancy Bush and *Slip-stitch Knitting* by Roxana Bartlett. You will also find useful books on specific techniques or pieces (e.g. toys, tea-cosies, etc.) at Search Press and Schoolhouse Press.

KNITTING BLOGS
Knitter's Review by Clara Parkes. www.knittersreview.com
Needled by Kate Davies. http://textisles.com

RESOURCES
The internet is an excellent resource for knitters, whether you are looking for videos explaining how to cast on or yarn suppliers. Here are some tips on how to find Blacker Yarns as well as your local pure wool suppliers. Blacker Yarns were used for all the projects in this book. If you want to use other yarns – including ones you have spun yourself – you must adjust the tension and pattern as necessary. Our website features the additional designs featured in this book and more: www.blackeryarns.co.uk or contact me at info@ blackeryarns.co.uk.

Single-breed yarns are also made by companies including R.E. Dickie (www. britishwool.com); Jamieson & Smith (www. shetlandwoolbrokers.co.uk); and Rowan Yarns (www.knitrowan. com).

To find suppliers local to you, or yarn from a particular breed, look on the internet for specific breed societies, farms or smallholdings, spinneries, farm shops, and agricultural, sheep or wool shows. Many farmers have blogs which will bring you closer to the farm and yarn producer. .

Creative Ewe knitting kits using Blacker Yarns www. blackerdesigns.co.uk

Ravelry A great place to meet likeminded knitters and research pure wool yarns. www.ravelry.com.

Index

Acknowledgements

Picture credits

We would like to thank the following for their kind permission to reproduce their photographs: **Alison Casserly** 38; **Amanda Crawford** 55; **Amanda Jones** 48; **British Wool Marketing Board** 6 bl, 12 bl, 15, 16 br, 20, 25, 32, 44, 46 br, 67, 75, 96, 101, 103, 109, 115, 131 br; **Diana Alderson** 80; **Diana Steriopolis** 14, 89; **Dominic Heneghen** 52, 54; **Douglas Bence** 7, 19 br, 112, 117 br; **iStock** 8 bl, br, 9 bl, 10 bl, 11 tr, 132, 134 bl, 138; **Jane Dansie** 123; **Jennie Martin** 49; **John Eveson** 9 br, 58; **Julie Halliday** 1, 39; **Karen Marshalsay** 127; **Linda Lunn** 79; **Myra Mortlock** 36; **Rita Taylor** 65; **Sam Morgan Moore** 2, 3, 4, 6 br, 8 background, 13 tl, 13tr, 16 c, 17, 18 background, bl, br, 19 bl, bc, 21 inset, 22, 23, 24, 26 inset, 27, 28, 30, 33 inset, 34, 35, 40 inset, 41, 42, 43, 45 inset, 46 bl, bc, 47, 49, 50, 51, 53 inset, 55, 57 59 inset, 60, 61, 62, 64, 65, 66, 68 inset, 69, 70, 72, 73, 76 inset, 77, 78, 79, 81 inset, 82, 83, 85, 86, 88, 90 inset, 91, 92, 97 inset, 98, 99, 102 inset, 10, 104, 110 inset, 111, 116 inset, 117 cr, 118, 119, 122, 124 inset, 125, 126, 130 background, bl, br, 131 bl, tr, 136; **Sarah Shourie** 72; **Sasha Kagan** 118; **Sian Brown** 126; **Simon Pask** 21, 26, 33, 40, 45, 53, 59, 68, 76, 81, 90, 97, 102, 110, 116, 124; **Tina Barrett** 31, 131 bc; **Vampy** 56.

Abbreviations: bl bottom left, br bottom right, c center, tl top left. tr top right.

Author's acknowledgments

I would like to thank the everyone who has contributed to this book. The photographers Sam Morgan Moore, Douglas Bence, Diana Alderson, Diana Steriopolis, Dominic Heneghen, John Eveson, Simon Pask and Julie Halliday; models Andrea, Katie, James, Finley, Sam and Miles; all the designers and knitters; and the patient editor and designer Julie Brooke and Louise Turpin.

I have written this book by standing on the shoulders of giants, people such as Robert Bakewell, who created the modern Leicester breed and Jo Henson, who saved the Castlemilk Moorit from extinction. I have also consulted the work of specialist writers of much more detailed, informative and better researched books on wool and yarns, a selection of which are listed in the bibliography.

I owe a debt to my mother who loved wool cloth, and probably taught me to knit (I cannot actually remember learning to knit, although I remember learning to read and write) and who knitted all our pullovers; to my own Ambler ancestors, who by working in the worsted trade in Bradford led me to understand that running a wool mill is a possibility; to Barbara Willis and Jane Deane who taught me to spin, and to the many in the wool trade, particularly Bob Armitage, Richard Brown and Robert Hirst, who, despite their misgivings about a woman starting a wool mill in Cornwall, have been unfailingly supportive.

I must also thank my whole family and the many friends, but especially Douglas my husband and Sam our son, for putting up with the whole sheep and wool obsession, looking after the sheep, modelling the clothes, picking up the pieces, cooking the meals, and helping to drink the wine.